The Basset Hound

Vintage Dog Books
Home Farm
44 Evesham Road
Cookhill, Alcester
Warwickshire
B49 5lJ

www.vintagedogbooks.com

ISBN No. 978-1-4067-9116-7

British Library Cataloguing-in-publication Data
A catalogue record for this book is available
from the British Library.

Vintage Dog Books
Home Farm
44 Evesham Road
Cookhill, Alcester
Warwickshire
B49 5lJ

www.vintagedogbooks.com

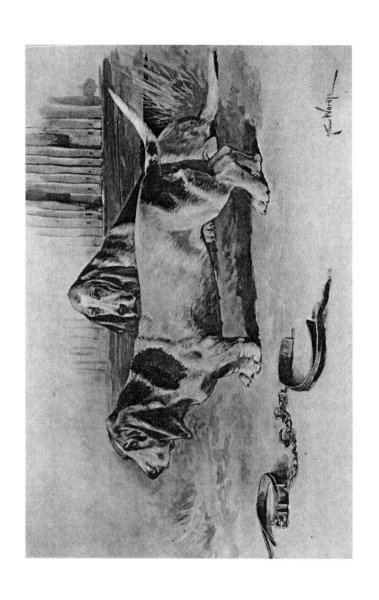

THE BASSET-HOUND.

In this handsome hound we have another example of the naturalisation of a foreign dog in this country. A quarter of a century ago he was a great favourite in France, and some other parts of the Continent, where he for years had been bred with great care; in England he was almost unknown. Now he is one of our own varieties, at least he is claimed as such, and even " Stonehenge," so loth to adopt anything for ourselves that did not belong to us, so far back as 1881, gave him a place amongst his " Dogs of the British Isles." The Kennel Club acknowledged him in their stud-book by classification in 1883, when but ten entries were made; there were thirty-eight in 1891 ; and the Curzon Hall committee at Birmingham moved the Basset from the variety class to one of its own in 1882.

Mr. Everett Millais, who took the initiative with regard to the Basset's introduction in this country, supplies me with the following valuable history and particulars of this hound :

" Before I commence a description of the various kinds of Bassets and their especial points, it might be advantageous to touch upon the origin of the word Basset, since it has been my misfortune, not once but many times, to listen to the most absurd reasons for the nomenclature of the hound. Briefly the word basset means ' a low thing ' or a ' dwarf,' and it has a similar derivation to the words bassinette, basset (the game), bastard, basse (a shoal), and many others which it is unnecessary for me to give, all of which have a common ancestor in the French adjective ' bas.'

" The meaning, then, of the word being almost apparent on the face of it, notwithstanding the fact that I have heard people urge with the greatest gravity that the Basset is a hound used for the purpose of hunting the basset, in the same way that the foxhound pursues the fox. It might also be interesting to observe how the hound became a dwarf, for if it be a dwarf, and this is what its name undoubtedly implies, it is obvious that it must be a dwarf of some other race of hound.

" It is also obvious that as there exist many varieties of Bassets in France, Belgium, Austria, and Germany, they too are dwarfs of some form of hounds.

" To account for this somewhat extraordinary assumption I must go back in the history of these countries to somewhat remote periods, and ask the reader what the use in those days, that is to say the days when men did not take the trouble to hunt small game, and the modern weapons of sport were still uninvented, would have been for such a hound as the Basset, which to-day, in France and Belgium especially, is looked upon as one of the best companions the sportsman can have by him.

" I need hardly say that such a hound as the Basset, when men followed the chase on horseback and looked upon rabbits and hares as vermin, would have been quite out of place, and the only logical conclusion one can come to as to the origin of these hounds is, that as men took up the chase of the smaller game a slower hound was required—a type of hound which would at once be produced by breeding only from those that were short in the leg, and consequently slower in speed. Breeding from such hounds, it must be observed, would but tend to decrease the height, and not the bodily proportions, coat, or form of head.

" In due time, as weapons made their appearance —and by weapons I especially mean when guns came into use—a slower dog still was required, which would either hunt in front of the sportsman or drive game slowly towards him.

" This type of hound would be produced by again breeding from the lowest and heaviest of his predecessors, and, what with the weight in front and the question of stability, the internal ligaments of the carpus would give way, the fore-feet would turn out so as to act as buttresses to the chest wall, and in the animal thus produced we should find a hound of full-sized body, of similar head and colour to the hounds from which it sprang, identical in fact with them except in this peculiar formation of the front and hind feet.

" Such undoubtedly is the manner in which the Basset originated, and what is still more remarkable is the fact that the tallest of the Bassets are the straight-legged ones, the medium the half-crooked, and the lowest the full-crooked, thus showing alone the gradual change which has been wrought by man to bring the great *chiens courants* down to the dwarfs or the Bassets of to-day.

" Had this manufacture, as I may reasonably call it, been limited to one breed of hound, we should naturally find but one breed of Bassets, but this is not so, since from the great variety of Bassets to be found in the countries I have named, it is certain that many breeds of hounds have been thus dealt with.

"As a result Bassets abroad are to be found smooth in coat, wire-haired and rough, straight-legged, half-crooked and full-crooked, and had we imported and bred all the varieties together, my task of describing them would have been somewhat difficult. I am glad, however, to say that we have stuck pretty closely to one strain in the smooths, and am in hopes that the same will follow in the Griffons, consequently in classifying them as we have them, or had them in this country, for one of the smooths has all but disappeared, I can name them as the Basset Français, and the Basset Griffon, the former being the smooth coated and the latter rough.

"In France every smooth-coated Basset is called a Basset Français, whether it be big, little, straight-legged or crooked, tricolour, lemon and white, or any hound colour whatever. The two strains which have been imported into this country are those which combine size with lowness in front and crook, tricolour or lemon and white markings, and, what is more to the point, the true hound type of those hounds from which they are descended. These two strains are the Le Couteulx and The Lane, originating respectively in the 'Artois' and 'Poitevin.'

"The strain of the Le Couteulx hounds owes its

origin to Mons. Le Comte le Couteulx le Cantalan, of Château St. Martin, near Etrepagny, one of the foremost sportsmen and the acknowledged authority on hunting and kennel matters in France, and from him takes its name.

" In it we find two modern types, both due to two hounds, viz., Fino de Paris, formerly the property of the Count, and Termino, the property of Mons. Masson—both of which I shall have to speak of again ; but as the difference between them is but of small importance, I will give a general outline of the type of the strain first, and revert to the small differences between them afterwards.

" In general appearance the Le Couteulx is a good sized hound, generally tricolour, but not uncommonly lemon and white, of heavy build and set on short legs, the fore ones being exceedingly massive and crooked.

" Taking the various portions of his body in order, we find the head to be large and set gracefully on the neck, which should be somewhat arched; the head should be domed, of considerable length, and narrow in comparison with its length, though far from weak. It should be of great depth, and the sides should be clean cut and free from any appearance of, or inclination to, cheek bumps.

" The nose should be inclined to the Roman type,

and be set on in a line with the external occipital protuberance, any dipping of a pronounced type or stop being unsightly. The nose itself should be strong and free from snipiness, while the teeth of the upper and lower jaws should meet. A pig-jawed hound, or one that is underhung, being distinctly objectionable.

" The lips should be square and not cut sharply away, and from the lower jaw extensive flews should fall towards the throat.

" The eye should be deeply sunken, showing a prominent haw, and in colour they should be a deep brown.

" The ears should be set on low; are of great length, of velvety texture, and should curl gracefully inwards ; their outer surface coming towards the base in contact with the side of the cheek and neck.

" The whole of the head should be covered with loose skin, so loose in fact, that when the hound brings its nose to the ground the skin over the head and cheeks should fall forward and wrinkle sensibly. In a word, the head of the Basset should resemble and approach as nearly as possible the bloodhound in conformation. The neck is massive but graceful, and as it approaches the body it thickens.

" The body itself is extremely powerful, and shows

as it is united with the sacrum a graceful rise, which disappears at the base or set on of the tail.

" If the animal were not so low to the ground its body would not appear of such length as it appears to be. At the same time, it is a lengthy body, but well supported by ribs; and as the ribs cease and we approach the sternum or chest, we find this to be capacious and of great width, the superior portion of the sternum standing out most prominently.

" The body of the chest comes right down between the fore-legs, fitting tightly in an angle formed by the approximation of the two radial bones, which are of great thickness. Below this point the carpus is straight, but the metacarpus inclines outwards, and the phalanges or toes completely so.

" In not a few specimens the carpus inclines forwards, thus giving the animal the appearance of knuckling over, which is a decided fault, and this is due largely to a forward inclination of the radius and ulna bones, which ought to incline inwards, and fit closely to the chest wall. On looking at the animal from the front we at once observe why the legs assume this peculiar formation, viz., inclining inwards from the elbow joint to the wrist joint, and then outwards again to the end of the toes.

" If the legs of the heavy Le Couteulx were straight

the chest would hang between, and the whole weight of the body would necessarily be centred at the shoulder joint. Consequently the animal would be incapable of any active movement and much exposed to dislocation at that joint; but as the legs incline inwards and then outwards the weight of the body is supported below the chest, viz., at the carpus, the latter being as it were the keystone on which the entire weight of the body falls. As a result it is at this point we should expect to find trouble if any portion of the architecture was out of position. I have drawn particular attention to the anatomy of the Bassets here, for it is at this joint we discover unsoundness if present, the reason being, as I have previously observed, that the radius and ulna bones are thrown too far forward, and not placed or gathered sufficiently behind the spot where the whole weight of the body converges.

" To be absolutely sound and perfect in legs, the Basset ought to stand in front between two and three inches from the ground, and in such a manner that if a plummet were dropped from the set on of the neck right through the dog it would touch the ground between the toes, and in front of the carpus.

" The hind legs are massive, like those in front, and should stand well below the hound to bear the weight of the back portion of his body. They are very muscular, as may be expected, seeing the great weight in front which they have to propel.

" The tail is of considerable length and should be carried gaily, though not so as to curl over the back.

" Our most perfect Bassets of the present day are undoubtedly Mr. Muirhead's Forester, Mrs. Ellis's Paris, Xena, and Dr. Woodhead's Geraldine, and I regret much that I have not their weights and measurements. I shall, however, not be wrong in giving those of my old Model, who, though rather flat in skull and having badly hung ears, was otherwise as perfect a specimen in other particulars as I ever hope to see.

" Measurements, &c., at seven and a half years of age : Weight, 46lb. ; height at shoulder, 12 inches ; length from tip of nose to set on of tail, 32 inches ; length of tail, 11½ inches ; girth of chest, 25 inches ; girth of loin, 21 inches ; girth of head, 17 inches ; girth of fore-arm, 6½ inches ; length of head from tip of occiput to tip of nose, 9 inches ; girth of muzzle at midway, 9½ inches ; length of ears from tip to tip, 19 inches ; height from ground between fore-feet 2¾ inches.

" I think I have gone now pretty clearly through the points of the Basset as far as his bodily points are concerned, consequently there remain but his coat and colouring.

THE BASSET

HE French short-legged hound which in England has the compound name basset-hound has never been popular in America. Why there should be the addition of "hound" to the name is not easy to understand for in its native country it has always been simply the basset. The late Everett Millais was the first to introduce the dog in England and wrote the description of the breed for Shaw's "Book of the Dog." So far as it went his description was good enough, but he made no attempt to go into old history. Buffon describes it and names two varieties, which were the crooked and the straight-legged types. But Millais makes the mistake of saying that the latter were the *petit chiens courant*, or small running hound. The probability is that these dogs were descendants from the old breed of greffiers, the dogs bred from the white St. Hubert hounds and the hound from Italy, or else from the St. Hubert hounds direct. These were dogs used on the liam and it is easy to understand that a dog which held its nose low to the ground by reason of its short legs would be preferred to one which had to make an effort to get his nose as low. We are very much of the opinion that the basset is the dog most entitled to be considered a direct descendant of the dogs which the Abbots of St. Hubert had to contribute annually to the king's kennels and which were used mainly for tracking on the liam. Buffon and other old French authorities held that the crooked legs were the result of rickets. In the "Dictionairre d'Historie Naturelle" it was stated that the crooked-legged variety were esteemed the best and that this originated in a malady similar to "*rachitis*" which was transmitted as a deformity to their descendants. It was finally held to be indicative of purity as we find in "La Chasse au Tir," Paris, 1827:—

"Deux Bassets bien dressés, Médor avec Brissant
........................Leur baroque structure
Vous announce déjà qu'ils sont de race pure."

As all abnormally long-bodied and short-legged dogs have a tendency to crooked forelegs in order to get balance, there is no reason to believe that the basset got his crooked legs from rickets any more than neglected short-legged dogs, where selection of straight legs is made essential, become bad fronted when selection is not attended to.

Colonel Thornton on his visit to France at the close of the eighteenth century saw these bassets and called them bloodhounds, described how they were led in tracking game to their resting places, and the one illustrated in his book he bought at the St. Germains kennels and took to England with him.

Mr. Millais introduced the basset to English dog shows in 1875, but it was not until Wolverhampton show of 1880 that they got their real start there. At that show Mr. Millais made a large entry and they attracted great attention. The late George R. Krehl then took up the breed and it became slightly popular, on account of its quaintness, and "There is such a lot to breed for," Mr. Krehl explained. This difficulty in breeding good dogs caused many to give them up in England, and except at the large shows the basset is relegated to the variety classes.

In America very few have been shown. Occasionally a new hand gets a brace or two and secures classes at New York show and then drops out after a brief trial. Mr. Higginson was the last to try them and got two couples of the rough variety to see whether they would not do as well as the beagles used by the Middlesex Hunt of Massachusetts, but they did not give satisfaction and the hunt graduated to English foxhounds.

The simplest way to describe the basset is to say he is a large dachshund with a head much like a bloodhound. The illustrations we give are sufficient to show what the dog was and now is without any descriptive particulars.

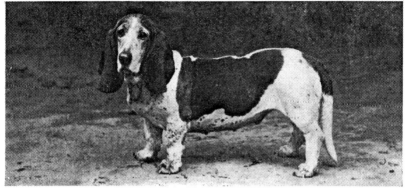

CH. QUEEN OF THE GEISHA
Owned by Mr. J. W. Proctor, England

Photograph by T. Fall, London

BASSETS
From a French publication of about 1840

Photograph by Baker, Birmingham

LOCKLY
Property of H. M. King Edward VII.

ROUGH BASSETS
Property of Mr. A. H. Higginson,
So. Lincoln, Mass.

FRENCH HOUND
Purchased by Colonel Thornton during his tour in
France in 1802 and called by him a "limier or blood-
hound," but in French a *briquet*. See page 597

OUNDS form a very large section of the dog family, as the term embraces all dogs which follow game either by sight or by scent. Of the former section the leading member of the present time is the greyhound, and has as its consorts the Irish wolfhound, the Scottish deerhound and the Russian wolfhound. To these may be added the later-made breed for racing and rabbit coursing, called the whippet or snap dog. Of the hounds that follow the quarry by scent we have the bloodhound, foxhound, harrier, beagle and basset; and up to a short time ago there was another variety of large foxhound called the staghound or buckhound, which was used in deer hunting, such as the Royal hunt after carted deer, or after wild deer in some of the still remaining sections of England where they were to be found. The Royal buckhounds were given up some years ago and the carted-deer hunts having fallen into disrepute as had the annual cockney Epping Hunt. Staghounds are not a breed of to-day nor, indeed, are harriers to the extent they were. The harrier is the intermediate dog between the foxhound and the beagle and has been interbred at each end, so that we have foxhound-harriers and beagle-harriers; and the old type of true harrier is confined to a very few English hunts and is not in any sense an American breed, though some small foxhounds in Canada are called harriers or "American foxhounds" as the owner pleases.

Lieutenant-Colonel Hamilton Smith, whose researches into the origin of the dog and the individual breeds have never been properly recognised by modern writers, to whom his work seems to have been unknown, devoted much attention to the question of the early hounds. When he wrote regarding ancient dogs researches in Assyria had not progressed so far as they had in Egypt, and he was only aware of one representation of a long-eared dog, the others being erect-eared. He was therefore inclined to the opinion that the greyhound type was the older. Since his day, however, we have had the Layard researches and those of later times and the pendulous-eared dog was the prevailing one in Assyria, according to sculptures and tablets which have been discovered there. A large number of the Egyptian hunting dogs were also drop-eared and any priority which may be claimed as between the greyhound or tracking hound will have to be based upon some other ground than description of ears.

In old Egyptian and Assyrian representations of dogs we have to take into consideration the conventional type, which differed very much. All Assyrian dogs are stout, strong, muscular dogs of what we should call mastiff type. The Egyptian artists, on the other hand depicted their dogs as leggy, light of build and running more to the greyhound type, "weeds" we would be likely to call them. We know that Assyrian dogs were taken to Egypt as gifts and also as tribute, yet these tribute dogs are painted on Egyptian conventional lines, while the same type of dogs by an Assyrian sculptor are made altogether different. We must therefore discard all of them as truly representative, except where we come across radical differences between Egyptian dogs or between dogs of Assyria.

It was Colonel Hamilton Smith's opinion that, although Greek and Roman authors gave tribal names to some sixteen or seventeen hunting dogs there were but two distinct races: one of greyhounds and one of dogs that hunted by scent. One of these tribal names was the Elymaean, which name was claimed by some to have come down through many generations in one form or another till it became the limer, the bloodhound led in leash or liam to track the quarry to its lair or harbour. There seems also to have been a dog of greyhound type that had a similar name, but with an added "m," its mission being to race at the game and pin it by the nose, whereas the bloodhound was not used further than to locate the game and was never off the lead. In the Assyrian sculptures we find hunting dogs on the lead and they are also represented in a similar manner in Egyptian paintings, both erect- and drop-eared, or, as we would characterise them, greyhounds and scenting hounds. There is nothing in which custom is more of an heirloom than in sporting practice and the leading of the greyhounds in slips, taking the brace of setters on lead, or coupling the hounds, might possibly have had its origin a long way farther back than the Assyrian dog on the leash which Layard considered was one of the oldest tablets he had found at Nineveh. It is only about two hundred years since foxhounds were hunted in couples, and all through the old prints and illustrations hounds are shown in couples when led afield, one man taking each couple.

The Hound Family

There is no reason to question the statement that the hounds originated in the Far East and followed the western migration, or accompanied it along the Mediterranean to Spain and to Ireland, likewise across Europe, leaving the Russian wolfhound's ancestors a little farther west than they did those of the Persian greyhound; dropping the Molossian for Greeks to admire and taking more of the same breed as they spread over Europe, to give to Spain the alaunt and to Germany and Denmark the Great Dane. With them came also the tracking hound and the swift racing dog, developed by centuries of breeding for speed till it became what it is to-day: the perfection of lines with but one object in view.

In the very oldest Greek and Latin books, we find that fads of fancy then existed and certain colours were valued more than others, the highest esteemed being the fawn or red with black muzzle, the colour the late Robert Fulton always maintained was the true bulldog colour and known to us as the red smut, or the fallow smut, according to the shade.

Other colours referred to by Xenophon are white, blue, fawn, spotted or striped; and they ranked according to individual fancy, just as they did for many hundreds of years. It was not until about Markham's time that we find authors discrediting colour as a guide to excellence or defect.

How much original relationship existed between the smooth greyhound and the other racing dogs is something which has been taken for granted and not looked into very closely. The Persian and Russian are the same dog, undoubtedly. So also the Irish wolfhound and the Scottish deerhound, while the smooth greyhound differs from the others as they also differ between themselves. Because they are much alike in shape is not to our mind sufficient evidence upon which to say that they are the same dogs changed by climatic influences, as Buffon held. Buffon maintained that a dog taken to a cold country developed in one direction, while a similar dog sent to a warm climate produced something quite different. Size, conformation, and coat were all changed, according to that authority, and he gave the French matin credit for being the progenitor of a large number of breeds upon that supposition. Climate has influence beyond a doubt, but there are other things just as important, one of which is selection. As far back as men knew anything they must have known that the way to get fast dogs was to breed fast dogs together; and if in eight generations it is possible to completely breed out a bulldog cross on a greyhound, as we shall show later on was accomplished, what is to prevent men all over the world taking any kind of medium-sized dogs and breeding them into greyhounds in shape, and eventually approaching them in speed ? We have an instance to hand in the Irish wolfhound, which was extinct, yet by crossing Danes and deerhounds a dog of the required type was produced in a very few years. Whippets are the production of about thirty years of breeding between terriers of various breeds, crossed with Italian greyhounds and small greyhounds—and what is more symmetrical than a whippet of class ?

The very name of greyhound is to our mind proof that this dog was originally a much smaller and very ordinary dog. Efforts have been made to prove that the greyhound was the most highly valued of all the dogs, hence and in keeping therewith a high origin was necessary for the word grey. According to some it was a derivation from Grew or Greek hound; Jesse held that "originally it was most likely grehund and meant the noble, great, or prize hound." Caius held that the origin of the word was "Gradus in latine, in Englishe degree. Because among all dogges these are the most principall, occupying the chiefest places and being absolutely the best of the gentle kinde of houndes." Mr. Baillie Grohman thinks the probable origin was grech or greg, the Celtic for dog, this having been the suggestion of Whitaker in his "History of Manchester." We can see but one solution of the name and that is from grey, a badger.

There was far more badger hunting than hare hunting when England was overrun with forests and uncultivated land, and a small dog for badgers would have earned his name as the badger hound or "grey" hound. Contemporaneous with this dog was the gazehound, which ran by sight, and, as terriers became a more pronounced breed and "grey" hounds found a more useful field of operations, the latter were improved in size and became classed with the gazehound as a sight hunter, eventually crowding out the older name of the coursing dog. That is our solution, and there is no wrenching a person's imagination with the supposition that Latin was the common language of Britain at the early period when this name was adopted.

We find a very similar substitution of name in the scenting hounds. The term harrier has for so long been associated with the sport of hare hunting that it is common belief that the dog got his name from the hare. A study of Caius would have caused some doubt as to that, for he only names the bloodhound and harrier as hounds of scent. The harrier was the universal hunting dog of his day, being used for the fox, hare, wolf, hart, buck, badger, otter, polecat, weasel, and rabbit. They were also used for the "lobster," a very old name for the stoat or martin; but this not being known to a French sporting author, he undertook to instruct his fellow countrymen how to catch rabbits by putting a crawfish into the burrows, having first netted all exits. The crawfish was supposed to crawl in till he got to the rabbits and then nip them till they made a bolt into one of the nets. If we did not have the French book with the instructions in we would feel inclined to doubt the truth of this story, to which, if we mistake not, we first saw reference in one of Colonel Thornton's books.

The meaning of harrier was originally to harry, to rouse the game, and had no reference to hares at all, it being more in regard to deer. In an Act of Parliament of one of the Georges this meaning is given to the name harrier, and was ridiculed in a sporting dictionary of about 1800. From the old spelling of the word, or the variety of methods of spelling it, there is ample evidence that the writers made no attempt to connect the dog with the hare. The Duke of York writes of "heirers," and other spellings are hayrers, hayreres, herettoir, heyrettars, herettor, hairetti. It will be noted that four of these spellings have "e" as the first vowel, while at that time the word hare was always spelt with an "a"; the spelling of harrier then began to change, and "a" replaced the "e" as the first vowel, and when harrier became thoroughly established the name eventually became more associated with the hounds specially kept for hare hunting until it was given to no other, and it finally became accepted that the harrier was a dog kept for hare hunting, and presumably always had been. That is something we can trace, but the probable transfer of the name of the badger dog to the hare courser is something that must have taken place years before writing was used to any extent in England.

The old name for running hounds in common use in Europe was brach in one of its many forms. Shakespeare uses the term several times, such as "I had rather hear Lady, my brach, howl in Irish." "Mastiff, greyhound, mongrel grim, hound or spaniel, brach or lym." Mr. Baillie Grohman gives the quotation from "Taming of the Shrew" as follows:—"Huntsman, I charge thee, tender well my hounds, brach Merriman—the poor cur is embossed," but it is now generally held that it should be "trash Merriman—the poor cur is embossed," otherwise, "take care of Merriman, the poor dog is tired out."

Nathaniel Cox, whose "Gentleman's Recreation" went through several editions from 1674 to 1721, gives "rache" as the latest rendering of the word.

The Dog Book

Cox is exceedingly unreliable as an authority, because he copied wholesale from old authors, with only a few alterations of his own. In the quotation referred to he says there were in England and Scotland but "two kinds of hunting dogs, and nowhere else in all the world." These are specified as the rache, with brache as feminine, and the sleuth hound. Here he differs from Caius who gives rache as the Scottish equivalent for the English brache.

Cox copied from some author the statement that the beagle was the gazehound, yet he describes the latter exactly as Caius did, stating that it ran entirely by sight and was "little beholden in hunting to its nose or smelling, but of sharpness of sight altogether, whereof it makes excellent sport with the fox and hare." That most assuredly does not fit the beagle yet a little further on he says, "After all these, the little beagle is attributed to our country; this is the hound which in Latin is called Canis Agaseus, or the Gaze-hound." This is not the agasseus which Oppian states was "Crooked, slender, rugged and full-eyed" and the further description of which fits the Highland terrier much better than the beagle, as we have already set forth in the chapter on the Skye terrier.

Cox credits the greyhound as an introduction from Gaul, but if such was the case they must have been greatly improved in size, or the dogs of the continent must have greatly deteriorated. Quite a number of illustrations of continental greyhounds are available to show the size of the levrier of France and Western Europe, and they all show dogs of the same relative size as those so well drawn in the painting by Teniers of his own kitchen. A hundred years later we have Buffon giving us the height at the withers of the levrier as 15 inches, which is just whippet size.

We have said nothing as to the bloodhound, which is another of those breeds about which there has been a good deal of romance. Originally the bloodhound was the dog lead on leash or liam, variously spelled, to locate the game. An example of the method is shown in the illustration facing page 284, the head and neck of the deer which is being tracked showing very plainly in the thicket close by. The dog having tracked the game to the wood was then taken in a circle around the wood to find whether exit had been made on the other side. If no trace was found the game was then said to be harboured and to this point the huntsmen and hounds repaired later for the hunt. These limers were selected from the regular pack, not on account of any particular breeding, but for their ability to track the slot of the deer, boar, or wolf. This use as slot trackers resulted in the name of

DEERHOUND
By Sir Edwin Landseer

FOXHOUND
By Charles Hancock

GREYHOUND
By A. Cooper

HARRIER
By A. Cooper

BLOODHOUND
By Charles Hancock

BEAGLE
By A. Cooper

TYPICAL HEADS
From the "Sportsman's Annual," 1836

sleuth hounds being given to them on the Scottish border. Naturally, in the case of wounded animals breaking away and trace of them being lost, these good-nosed dogs found further employment in tracking the quarry by the blood trail, and here we have the bloodhound name. It was ability, not breeding, that caused a dog to be drafted as a limer or bloodhound, and we cannot show this more conclusively, perhaps, than by jumping to the "Sporting Tour" of Colonel Thornton in France in 1802. In describing wild boar hunting he says: "A huntsman sets his bloodhound upon the scent and follows him till he has reared the game." He purchased one of these hounds, which had been bred at Trois Fontaines and illustrated it in his book and it proves to be a basset. Here we have the name applied, as it always had been, to the use the dog was put to and not to the specific breed of the dog. Colonel Thornton, in speaking more particularly of this special dog, said that the breed name was *briquet*.

The prevalent opinion is that the bloodhound is a descendant from what has been called the St. Hubert hound, and in support of this contention the favourite piece of evidence is Sir Walter Scott's lines:

"Two dogs of black St. Hubert's breed,
Unmatched for courage, breath, and speed."

The legend is that in the sixth century, St. Hubert brought black hounds from the South of France to the Ardennes, and it is supposed that these hounds came from the East. It was also said that some white hounds were brought from Constantinople, by pilgrims who had visited Palestine, and on their return they offered these dogs at the shrine of St. Roch, the protecting saint from hydrophobia. These dogs were also called St. Hubert hounds and it is stated that the white dogs were the larger and more prized of the two. The Abbots of St. Hubert gave six hounds annually to the king and it was from these hounds that the best limers were said to be obtained.

If we are to accept later-day poetical descriptions as conclusive evidence, then the St. Hubert hounds were magnificent animals, with all the characteristics of the modern show bloodhound, and with a deep, resounding voice. Records are not made in that fanciful way and what evidence we have is to the effect that the St. Hubert was a heavy, low, short-legged dog, running almost mute and particularly slow in movements. In fact, we are very much of the opinion that the basset is the descendant of the St. Hubert breed. As evidence in that direction, we present an extract from that exceedingly scarce work, the "Sportsman's Annual" for 1839. Who the editor was we have not been able to ascertain, but it contains a dozen beautifully executed and coloured dogs' heads drawn specially for this number, seemingly the first of what was to be an annual, but which was only issued the one year. We reproduce a number of the heads of the hounds, by Landseer, Hancock, and Cooper; that of the harrier by the later being, in our opinion, the most beautifully executed head of any dog we have ever seen.

In the letterpress regarding the bloodhound we find the following extract credited to "a small quarto volume of fifteen pages, printed in 1611, and very scarce":

"The hounds which we call St. Hubert's hounds, are commonly all blacke, yet neuertheless, their race is so mingled in these days that we find them of all colours. These are the hounds which the Abbots of St. Hubert haue always kept, or some of their race or kind, in honour or remembrance of the saint, which was a hunter with S. Eustace. Whereupon we may conceiue that (by the Grace of God) all good huntsmen shall follow them into paradise. To returne unto my former purpose, this kind of dogges hath been dispersed through the countries of Henault, Lorayne, Flaunders, and Burgoyne. They are mighty of body, neuertheless their legges are low and short, likewise they are not swift, although they be very good of scent, hunting chaces which are farre stranggled, fearing neither water nor cold and doe more couet the chaces that smell, as foxes, bore, and like, than other, because they find themselues neither of swiftnes nor courage to hunt and kill the chaces that are lighter and swifter. The bloudhounds of this colour proue good, especially those that are cole-blacke, but I make no great account to breede on them or to keepe the kind, and yet I found a booke which a hunter did dedicate to a Prince of Lorayne, which seemed to loue hunting much, wherein was a blason which the same hunter gaue to his bloudhound, called Soullard, which was white, whereupon we may presume that some of the kind proue white sometimes, but they are not of the kind of the Greffiers, or Bouxes, which we haue at these days." The hound Soullyard was a white hound and was a son of a distinguished dog of the same name:

" My name came first from holy Hubert's race,
   Soullyard, my sire, a hound of singular grace. "

The Hound Family

The name of the author of the fifteen-page book is, unfortunately, not mentioned, but he was in error regarding the colour of the St. Huberts in the Royal kennels and that of the Greffiers, as he spells the name.

Another importation of hounds was made by St. Louis toward the middle of the thirteenth century, which are described as taller than the usual run of French hounds, and were faster and bolder than the St. Huberts. These were described as *gris de lievre*, which may be interpreted as a red roan. These hounds seem to have been extensively used as a cross on the low French hounds, but no importation seems to have had so much effect as that of the bracco, or bitch, brought from Italy by some scrivener or clerk in the employ of Louis XII. This Italian bitch was crossed with the white St. Huberts and her descendants were known as *chiens griffiers*. So much improvement did these dogs show that special kennels were built for them at St. Germains and they became the popular breed.

Specimens of all of these hounds undoubtedly went to England and we may also assume that English pilgrims and crusaders brought back dogs from the East as they did to France, the progeny of which were drafted as they showed adaptability or were most suited for the various branches of sport, but it is more than doubtful whether any hunting establishments in England approached the greater ones of France. The Duke of Burgundy had in his employ no less than 430 men to care for the dogs and attend to the hunts, hawking and fisheries. There was one grand huntsman, 24 attendant huntsmen, a clerk to the chief, 24 valets, 120 liverymen, 6 pages of the hounds, 6 pages of the greyhounds, 12 under pages, 6 superintendents of the kennels, 6 valets of limers, 6 of greyhounds, 12 of running hounds, 6 of spaniels, 6 of small dogs, 6 of English dogs (probably bulldogs), 6 of Artois dogs; 12 bakers of dogs' bread; 5 wolf hunters, 25 falconers, 1 net-setter for birds, 3 masters of hunting science, 120 liverymen to carry hawks, 12 valets fishermen and 6 trimmers of birds' feathers.

It will be seen, however, that only three varieties of hounds are named, and these were the lines of distinction set by Buffon, who named them levrier, chien courant and basset as the successors of what are named in the foregoing list as greyhounds, running hounds and limers. It is therefore to England we owe the perfection of the greyhound, the preservation of the deerhound, and the improvement and subdivision of the running hounds into foxhounds, harriers and beagles, together with the establishment of type in each variety.

CHAPTER XXII

THE BASSET-HOUND

SINCE the time of the gentleman who at one time wrote over the *nom de guerre* of "Snapshot," and who is better known to the present generation of doggy men as "Wildfowler," the Basset-hound has, in this country, attained to very considerable numerical strength. The fact that Mr. Everett Millais, when acting as judge at the show held at the Royal Aquarium, Westminster, in 1886, had 120 entries to deal with, shows that admirers of the breed have not been wanting; and that exhibition was in strong contrast to the time— not more than ten years before—when Lord Onslow and Mr. Everett Millais were the only exhibitors of these crook-legged, slow hounds, and had to show them in the *omnium gatherum* class, which may be described as the show committee's finest-mesh net, that secures all the fish and finance that escape the regulation nets.

Though it will be necessary to take a closer view of the Basset in England since his introduction into this country, yet the following remarks, contributed by "Wildfowler" to the original edition of this work, are so interesting that they merit reproduction.

"Snapshot" was a frequent contributor, under that signature, to the *Country*, and was also well known as "Wildfowler" of the *Field*; he was the author of numerous canine articles and works, including "General Sport at Home and Abroad," "Modern Wild-fowling," etc. His experience with Continental sporting dogs was considerable, which gives weight and value to his article on Bassets. He says :—

"Any hound which stands lower than 16in. (no matter his 'provincial' breed) is called in France and in Belgium a Basset. The derivation of the expression Basset is clear: *bas* means low; and, therefore, Basset means low set, a very appropriate denomination as applied to these diminutive hounds.

The vast army of French and Belgian Bassets may be divided into three grand classes—viz. Bassets *à jambes droites* (straight-legged), ditto *à jambes demi-torses* (with fore legs half crooked), and ditto *à jambes torses* (fore legs fully crooked). And in each of these classes will be found three varieties of coats—viz. the Bassets *à poil ras* (smooth-coated), those *à poil dur* (rough-coated), and a class half rough, half smooth-coated, which is called half griffon.

The types vary for almost each province, but the general characteristics remain throughout pretty well the same. All well-bred Bassets have long, pendulous ears and hounds' heads ; but the crooked-legged breeds show always better points in these respects than the straight-legged ones, simply because, when a man wishes to breed a good Basset *à jambes torses*, he is obliged to be very careful in selecting the stock to breed from, if he does not wish his experiment to end in failure, for, should there be the slightest admixture of foreign blood, the 'bar sinister' will be at once shown in the fore-legs. Hence the Bassets *à jambes torses* show, as a rule, far better properties than their congeners.

In build the Basset *à jambes torses* is long in the barrel, and is very low on his pins ; so much so that, when hunting, he literally drags his long ears on the ground. He is the slowest of hounds, and his value as such cannot be over-estimated. His style of hunting is peculiar, inasmuch that he will have his own way, and each one tries for himself ; and if one of them finds, and 'says' so, the others will not blindly follow him and give tongue simply because he does (as some hounds, accustomed to work in packs, are apt to do) ; but, on the contrary, they are slow to acknowledge the alarm given, and will investigate the matter for themselves. Thus, under covert, Bassets *à jambes torses* following a scent go in Indian file, and each one speaks to the line according to his own sentiments on the point, irrespective of what the others may think about it. In this manner, it is not uncommon to see the little hounds, when following a mazy track, crossing each other's route without paying any attention to one another ; and, in short, each of them works as if he were alone. This style I attribute to their slowness, to their extremely delicate powers of scent, and to their innate stubborn confidence in their own powers. Nevertheless, it is a fashion which has its drawbacks ; for, should the individual hounds hit on separate tracks of different animals, unless at once stopped, and put together on the same one, each will follow its own find, and let the shooter or shooters do his or their best. That is why a shooter who is fond of that sort of sport rarely owns more than one or two of these hounds. One is enough, two may be handy in difficult cases, but more would certainly entail confusion, precisely because each one of them will rely only on the evidence of his own senses.

I have now several clever Bassets *à jambes torses* in my mind's eye, and their general description would be about as follows : Height, between 10in. and 15in. at shoulder ; longish barrels ; very crooked fore legs, with little more than an inch or two of daylight between the knees ; stout thighs ; gay sterns ; conical heads ; long faces ; ears long enough to overlap each other by an inch or two (and more sometimes) when both were drawn over the nose ; heavy-headed rather, with square muzzles ; plenty of flews and dewlap ; eyes deep set, under heavy wrinkles ; fore paws wide, and well turned out ; markings, hare-pied and white, black tan and white, tan and white, black with tan eyebrows, and tan legs and belly, etc.—in short, all the varieties of hound markings will be found among them. They have excellent tongues for their size, and when in good training and good condition they will hunt every day, and seem to thrive on it. They are very fond of the gun, and many are cunning enough to ' ring ' the game, if missed when breaking covert, back again to the guns until it is shot. Some of these Bassets are so highly prized that no amount of money will buy them ; and, as a breed, it may safely be asserted that it is probably the purest now in existence in France. They hunt readily deer, roebuck, wild boars, wolves, foxes, hares, rabbits, etc., but if entered exclusively to one species of quarry, and kept to it, they never leave it to run riot after anything else. I have seen one, when hunting a hare in a park, running through fifty rabbits and never noticing them. They go slowly, and give you plenty of time to take your station for a shot—hence their great value in the estimation of shooters. They are chiefly used for smallish woods, furze fields, and the like, because, if uncoupled in a forest, they do not drive their game fast enough ; and though eventually they are bound to bring it out, yet the long time they would take in so doing would tell against the sport. Moreover, large forests are cut about by ditches, and here and there streamlets, boulders, and rocks intervene, which difficulty the short, crooked-legged hound would be slow in surmounting. He is, therefore, not so often used there as for smaller coverts, where his voice can throughout the hunt be heard, and thereby direct the shooters which post of vantage to take.

As regards the coats of Bassets *à jambes torses*, there are both rough, half-rough, and smooth-coated specimens ; but the last two predominate greatly ; in fact, I have but rarely seen very rough Bassets *à jambes torses*. I saw three once, in the Ardennes. They were very big hounds for Bassets, and were used chiefly to drive wolves, roebuck, and wild boars. They were *à poil dur* with a vengeance, and, when ' riled,' their backs were up like bristles. Of course, in these matters the chasseurs breed their hounds according to the ground they have to hunt over; and, consequently, in provinces of comparatively easy coverts, such as vineyards, small woods, furze fields, etc., smooth-coated or half rough-coated Bassets are in universal demand. In Brittany, Vendée, Alsace, Lorraine, Luxemburg, on the contrary, wherever the coverts are extensive and very rough, rougher-coated hounds are used ; but *poil durs* are scarce, as far as diminutive hounds are concerned.

Bassets *à jambes demi-torses* are simply crosses between Bassets *à jambes torses* and Bassets *à jambes droites*. They are usually bigger than the former and smaller than the latter, although it must be borne in mind that there are several varieties of Bassets *à jambes droites* quite as small as the smallest with crooked legs. In short, there are so many subdivisions in each breed that any classification must necessarily be general.

The advantages claimed by the owners of Bassets *à jambes demi-torses* are these: first, these hounds are almost as sure-nosed as the full-crooked breeds; secondly, they run faster, and yet not fast enough to spoil shooting; thirdly, in a wood with moderate ditches, being bigger in body and higher on the leg than the full-crooked Bassets, they can clear the ditches at a bound, whereas the full *jambes torses* have to go down into them, and scramble up on the other side. In points, they are pretty much like their congeners, but already the cross tells. The lips are shorter ; the muzzle is not so stout in proportion to general size ; the ears are much shorter ; the skull is less conical, the occiput being not so pronounced ; the body is not so long ; the stern is carried more horizontally ; the feet are rounder ; the wrinkles in the face are fewer ; the eye is smaller ; and the coat, as a rule, is coarser. The increase in size is also great. I have seen such reaching to fully 16in. ; and I believe they had been obtained by a direct cross from a regular *chien courant* (hound) with a full Basset *à jambes torses*. When sire and dam are both good, there is no reason why the progeny should not answer the breeder's purpose ; but I confess to a tendency for either one thing or the other, and, were I to go in for fancy for that breed of hounds, I would certainly get either a thoroughly crooked Basset or a thoroughly straight-on-his-pins Beagle. By the way, a black-and-tan or a red Basset *à jambes torses* cannot, by any possible use of one's eyes, be distinguished from a Dachshund of the same colour, although some German writers assert that the breeds are quite distinct. To the naked eye there is no difference ; but in the matter of names (wherein German scientists particularly shine), then, indeed, confusion gets worse confounded. They have, say, a dozen black-and-tan Bassets *à jambes torses* before them. Well, if one of them is a thorough good-looking hound, they call him Dachs Bracken ; if he is short-eared, and with a pointed muzzle, they cap him with the appellation of a Dachshund. Between you and me, kind reader, it is a distinction without a difference, and there is no doubt that both belong to the same breed. I will, at a fortnight's notice, place a Basset *à jambes torses*, small size, side by side with the best Dachshund hound to be found, and if any difference in legs, anatomy, and general appearance of the two can be detected, I shall be very greatly surprised. That the longer-eared and squarer-muzzled hound is the better of the two for practical work there is not the shadow of a doubt ; but, of course, if digging badgers is the sport in view, then the Dachshund Terrier is the proper article. But that is not to be admitted. One cannot breed Hounds from Terriers, whereas one can breed Terriers from Hounds, and therefore the Dachshund Terrier is descended from the Basset *à jambes torses*. As for Dachshund hounds, they are, in every respect, Basset *à jambes torses* ; at least, that is the opinion I have come to after a great deal of experience. Quarrelling about names is an unprofitable occupation. Never mind the ' Bracken ' or the ' Hund,' since the two articles are alike. I say, from the evidence of my senses, that they must come from the same stock, and, since they cannot come from a Terrier pedigree, the Hound one is the only logical solution.

The Basset *à jambes droites* is synonymous with our Beagle ; but, whereas our Beagles rarely exceed 14in., it is not uncommon to see some Bassets reaching even 16in. in France ; still, it should be remembered that then, even among the French, appellations will differ. Thus, a certain school will call 16in. Bassets *petits chiens courants*, and will deny them the right of being called Bassets, being, in their estimation, too high on the leg. I agree with them. The characteristics of Bassets *à jambes droites* are—a somewhat shorter face than those with crooked legs ; ears shorter, but broader, and very soft usually ; neck a shade longer ; stern carried straight up ; good loins ; shorter bodies, very level from shoulder to rump : whereas the other two breeds are invariably a shade lower at shoulder than at the stern. Some show the *os occipitis* well marked ; others are more apple-headed ; the hair is coarse on the stern ; the feet are straight and compact, knees well placed, thighs muscular and well proportioned ; in short, they are an elegant-looking, dashing, and rather taking breed as a lot. But in work there is a world of difference. The crooked-legged ones go slow and sure ; the straight-legged ones run into the defect of fast hounds—*i.e.* they go too fast occasionally for their noses ; they are not, either, quite so free from riot ; but wherever pretty fast work is required, and when the covert requires some doing in the way of jumping drains and scrambling over boulders, etc., then they will carry the day. They are chiefly used for large game, in pretty large coverts, and run in small packs. For fast fun, exercise, and music, they will do ; but for actual shooting, commend me to the Basset *à jambes torses*. With such a little hound, if he knows you and understands your ways, you are bound to bag, and alone he will do the work of ten ordinary hounds ; and, in truth, there are few things more exciting to the sportsman than to hear his lonely, crooked-legged companion, merrily, slowly, but surely, bringing his quarry to his gun. Some of the pleasantest moments of my life have been thus spent ; and once, having shot two wolves that had been led out to me by a Basset *à jambes torses*, I fairly lifted up the little beggar to my breast and hugged him, and I called him a pet and a dear, and all that sort of bosh, and I thought that in all my life I had never seen a pluckier and cleverer little fellow.

In short, there is no doubt that, for purposes of shooting, Bassets, of whatever breed, are pre-eminently excellent. They run very true, and are more easily taught the tricks of game than full-sized hounds. This I have found out by experience. The average large hound, once in full swing on a scent, runs on like a donkey. But Bassets seem to reason, and when they come to an imbroglio of tracks, purposely left by the quarry to puzzle them, they are rarely taken in, but, slowly and patiently setting to work, they unravel the maze, and eventually pick up again the wily customer's scent. Hence, for the man who can only keep one or two hounds to be used with the gun, there is no breed likely to suit him better than Bassets, for they are sure not to lose the scent, whatever takes place, and their low size enables them to pick it up when it is so cold that a larger hound would, perhaps, not even notice it.

They have also a good deal of pluck, to which they add a sort of reasoning discretion. To illustrate my meaning, I will give an instance to the point—viz. very few hounds of any kind take readily to hunting wolves, and when they do take to it, they hunt in a pack, each hound countenancing the other. Now, some well-bred Bassets will hunt a wolf singly. I have stated already that I have had myself the pleasure of killing two wolves that were, individually, hunted by one Basset. This, therefore, shows extraordinary pluck on the part of the little hound ; for be it known that, as a rule, any hound or dog who comes for the first time on the scent of a wolf forthwith bolts home, or hides behind his master for protection. On the other hand, Bassets are cautious. When they by chance come near a wolf, or a wild boar, or a stag, or any other wild animal on whom they could make but little impression, but who is, on the other hand, likely to do them an irretrievable injury, they never run the risk, but bay at him from a distance. As long as he chooses to stop they will not leave him ; they will resume hunting him as soon as he will start, but they will only run at him when the decisive shot has been fired.

Some Bassets are used for vermin-killing (badger, fox, etc.) ; others are employed for pheasant-shooting, woodcock-shooting, and partridge-shooting, besides their legitimate employment in hunting ground game. When used for birds, they are frequently called to, to keep them within range, and, generally, a bell or a small brass *grelot* is fastened to their collar, that the shooter may know where they are. Some men make their Bassets retrieve, even from water; and most Bassets will go to ground readily to fox or badger.

Finally, some peasants use their extraordinary powers of scent to find truffles. Their training for that sort of business is wonderfully simple. The hound, when young, is kept a day without food, and a truffle being shown to him, the peasant throws it into some small covert, or hides it in stones, or buries it lightly in the ground, and makes the dog find it; when he has done so, he gives him a piece of bread—this sort of thing being repeated until the Basset looks readily for the truffle. He is then taken to those places in the neighbourhood of which truffles are known or suspected to be, and the peasant, pretending to throw away the usual truffle, tells the dog, ' *Cherchez!—cherchez!* ' ('Seek!—seek!'), whereupon the little hound, diligently ferreting about the ground, soon comes upon a truffle scent, and begins digging for the tuber. At the first sign of that process the peasant relieves him, and digs out the precious fungus; and so on. There are some other species of dogs also used for that sort of work; but the Basset, owing to his acute power of scent, is mostly preferred by the professional *chercheurs de truffes*. Some of these men, however, use pigs for the purpose.

Concerning those French Bassets which have from time to time been exhibited at our shows, some of them have shown fair points, but none of them have had the very long ears which one will notice with the Bassets in the foresters' kennels on the Continent. Moreover, in the classes set aside for Bassets, I do not remember having seen a good Basset *à jambes torses*, though there were one or two fair specimens of half-crooked and straight-legged Bassets. If my memory serves me right, the Earl of Onslow's were straight-legged, half rough-coated Bassets, with remarkably short ears. Mr. Millais' Model was a black, white, and tan, smooth-coated Basset, with very fair properties—the best I had seen in England so far—and a Vendéan Basset was a regular Griffon. I forget now the state of his legs, but his coat was just the sort of jacket for the rough woods of Brittany and Vendée.

On the other hand, in the classes for Dachshunds I have seen some first-rate black-and-tan and also red Bassets *à jambes torses*, all smooth-coated. No doubt, eventually, classes will be set apart for each individual breed, and in such a case there is a very fine field yet open for an enterprising exhibitor wishing to produce Bassets in open court."

Since the foregoing was written the Basset-hound has, by importation and breeding, greatly increased in this country; and

14

to all frequenters of shows this quaint animal, with his short, bandy legs and heavy body, has now become familiar; and a better knowledge of his intrinsic qualities has secured for him admirers, even among those who, on his first introduction, scoffed at him as a deformity, a disproportioned beast, with the clumsy gait and the abnormal strength often found in misshapen dwarfs.

This better acquaintance and closer study of the Basset have compelled a change in the view taken of the breed, and most unprejudiced persons are now ready to admit that these hounds possess characteristics worthy of the admiration of both the sportsman and the dog-lover; consequently, they are no longer looked

FIG. 52.—THE LATE SIR EVERETT MILLAIS'S SMOOTH BASSET MODEL.

upon—as when Mr. Millais first exhibited Model, at Wolverhampton, in 1875—as oddities or curiosities, only fit for a place in a museum of the *Canidæ*, and, as the rector's wife said of Di Vernon, "of no use in the 'varsal world."

There is reason for believing that the preceding article on the breed, contributed to the original edition of "British Dogs" by "Wildfowler," was a powerful incentive to that study of the Basset which has resulted in its becoming a recognised British breed.

Mr. Everett Millais (who died soon after succeeding to the title on the death of his father) imported Model in 1874, the portrait of which, drawn by Mr. R. H. Moore, from an oil painting by Sir J. E. Millais, R.A., is given with this chapter (Fig. 52). Mr. E. Millais was at that time under the impression that Model was the first of the breed imported, and that hound was certainly the first of his kind exhibited at an English dog show. It appears, however, from a pamphlet ("Bassets : their Use and Breeding") subsequently written and published by Mr. Millais, and to which it will be necessary to refer on several points, that Lord Onslow possessed, prior to Model's importation, several Bassets, which had been given to him by Lord Galway, who had been presented with them by Comte Tournon, of Montmelas. These are the first imported Bassets on record ; but it would be against fair inference from undoubted evidence to suppose that Bassets, like other French breeds, had not been brought to England centuries ago, although the blood has been absorbed and lost in the flood of other varieties. At the time, however, that Mr. Millais obtained Model, no other representative of the breed could be found in this country, and his owner, therefore, resorted to a Beagle cross, claiming that in the second generation he was able to show hounds at the Agricultural Hall in 1877 which it was impossible to distinguish from pure Bassets. He gave up this strain when Lord Onslow imported Fino and Finette from Comte le Couteulx, the breeder of Model.

The next great impulse towards popularising these hounds here was, undoubtedly, the importation of specimens from the best French kennels, by "Wildfowler" and Mr. G. R. Krehl; to a remarkable extent by the latter's Fino de Paris, a hound of great beauty and of concentrated pedigree, whose blood runs in the majority of Bassets of the day.

Fino de Paris deserves a few words to himself, so potent has his influence been upon the breed. Mr. Krehl showed excellent judgment in acquiring him in 1880. Mr. Millais, who could have had him at an earlier date, believed him to be Model's brother, but he had the bloodhound type of head to which we have bred since, while Model's was more on the lines of a Foxhound's. Now we may trace the foundation of the breed as it is to-day in Great Britain. The union of Model with Lord Onslow's Finette produced Garenne and Proctor. The latter, put to Juno, a bitch imported by Lord Onslow, produced Cigarette, who became the dam of Medore by Champion Bourbon (Fino de Paris ex Guinevere). The alliance of Medore with Fino VI. (a son of Fino V. by Vivien, a grand-daughter of Fino de Paris) resulted in the birth of Champions Forester, Fresco, Merlin, and Flora, all names of great moment in the Basset-hound world.

The next potent factor in the establishment of the breed in this country came into play in 1883. It is related of certain voyagers that, when in immediate danger of shipwreck, and it was found no one of their number was capable of conducting the devotions suitable to the perilous occasion, a brilliant idea presented itself to

one of them, who exclaimed : " Let us make a collection." In
the doggy world, when a breed does not prosper as its devotees
desire, some one possessed of specimens writes to the newspapers,
and says, " Let us form a club " ; and, calling a few friends together,
a club is formed, and a standard framed to match existing specimens, by which all future dogs of the breed are to be judged.

In 1883, then, the Basset Club was instituted, and the immense
increase of these hounds in England is largely due to its influence.
The Club proposed to itself the task of defining the true type, of
publishing a full and minute description of the breed, and also a
book of pedigrees. A fourth edition of the Stud Book (originally
compiled by Mr. Everett Millais) was published in 1900, having
been corrected and brought up to date by Mrs. Tottie.

Turning, for the time being, from this part of the subject to a
consideration of the uses of Bassets, it will be seen, from " Wildfowler's " contribution, that in France their chief use is in serving
the gun, and especially in driving ground game from the coverts to
the open glades, rides, or avenues, wherein the shooters take up
their position ; and although not kept exclusively to that work, yet
there is no mention of them being used as we do our Harriers and
Beagles.

At the time that Arrian lived hounds corresponding to the
modern Basset were used for hunting, as we use the term, many
centuries before " villainous saltpetre was digged out of the bowels
of the harmless earth " for the making of gunpowder. Such use
of hounds was an absolute necessity of the then existing circumstances ; and, no doubt, in times nearer to our own, Bassets
were also used to drive game within reach of the bowman's shaft
long before the " mimic thunder " of the iron tube roused the
echo, as it sounded the death of hare or pheasant.

Bassets are now employed to a considerable extent in hare-
hunting in this country, in packs, as Harriers are used, and, in
many instances, with marked success.

Mr. Fred. W. Blain, of Bromborough, Cheshire, well known
in the earlier days of the breed, wrote to the previous edition
of " British Dogs " :—

" During the past few years the number of Basset-hounds in
this country has greatly increased, and I am glad to see that
they are growing in favour as sporting dogs. For hare-hunting
they are excellent, and for some reasons I think they are preferable
to Beagles. They are by no means as slow as most people imagine,
and they will go on for hours at top speed, showing great endurance
and pluck. Like most delicate-nosed hounds, such as Bloodhounds,
Otter-hounds, and the old Southern Hounds, Bassets are inclined
to dwell very much on a scent, and to be rather too free with

their tongue ; they like to work out every inch of the trail, and, as they invariably cast *back* of their own accord, they hunt best when left pretty much to themselves. They should not be pressed, especially at the beginning, before they are well settled to their work.

It is well known that the formation of a fair pack of Foxhounds is the work of very many years, even with the great number of drafts to choose from. With Bassets, the number a buyer can select from is very limited—they vary greatly in size and build, and, of course, in speed ; yet some people, having got together half a dozen hounds of all sizes and shapes, never hunted before, and probably bred from parents which for generations have not done a day's hunting, are disgusted because they do not show good sport. Surely this is unreasonable. A certain amount of time and patience are required before a pack can be formed of, say, eight couple, well matched in speed, and hunting nicely together ; but with such a pack splendid results are obtained, and I have heard old Beagle men most enthusiastic in their praise. On a smaller scale very good amusement and exercise may be obtained with two couple or so, run on a plain rabbit-skin drag, or even merely letting them track their kennelman across country.

Let me advise any one trying Bassets for hunting not to attempt to teach them with the whip and harsh words, as they are very sensitive, and easily frightened, and in some cases never forget a thrashing. Headstrong they certainly are, and fond of their own way—but this failing must be put up with ; to those who know the breed they are not hard to manage, with a little tact.

I consider that, in making use of Bassets to run as Beagles, we are taking them rather out of their element, and, consequently, it will take time before they can be expected to be perfect at this work. For shooting where the coverts are too dense for beaters, Bassets in France take the place of our Spaniels, driving everything before them, and making such a noise that neither boar nor rabbit is likely to remain in cover. This was, I think, their original use in France ; but in this country game is generally too plentiful and highly preserved for them to be much used.

I hope that, in breeding Bassets for hunting purposes, owners will not neglect the heavy and somewhat ungainly appearance that they should have, and gradually get them higher on the leg and lighter in bone and body ; by so doing they may increase the speed, but they will lose the endurance, and they will in time be nothing better than deformed Beagles. I have already noticed a tendency in this direction in packs. If Bassets are not fast enough for a man, let him by all means keep Beagles instead. You cannot expect a Clydesdale to go as fast as a thoroughbred, nor would you think of breeding them to do so. Keep each to his real work : both are good, but their style may suit different tastes."

Lieutenant Munro was also the Master of a pack, which he regularly hunted, about the same period; but from a note of that gentleman, quoted by Mr. Millais, he appears rather to have used them to beat rabbits to the gun than as hare-hounds. Lieutenant Munro says : "Two years ago I had a very good pack of eight couple working hounds, all good hunting, and staunch. If one of my hounds gave tongue, I was certain that there was a rabbit. I used to shoot over my Bassets, and have often killed fifty couple rabbits a day over them. I believe, when bred carefully for this object, they are the *best* sort of dogs for rabbiting."

Speaking of the same hounds, Mr. Northcote, another well-known admirer of Bassets, says : " He [Mr. Munro] used them for rabbiting. I was delighted with them. Their lovely music, like a Foxhound ; first-rate nose ; and, after finding, keeping together in a pack after one rabbit, however many there were about—to me was enchanting, adding considerably to the sport."

Mr. T. Pick, who had the care and management of the Earl of Onslow's Bassets, and who continued to breed these hounds, writing at the time when the Earl of Onslow had just given up the breed, and made a present of most of his dogs to Mr. Pick, said :—

"They are the most intelligent dogs in the world. They are very keen hunters, and I have hunted a hare with them, with two inches of snow on the ground, for over two miles. I have also hunted a hare with them for a mile, over a dust-blown field, with a warm sun and a dry east wind, at four o'clock in the afternoon. Once, when out with a pup a few days under four months old, named Proctor, a rabbit crossed the gravel path, and when the pup came on the scent he immediately gave tongue, and followed up the scent for about 400 yards, when the rabbit got into his hole. That pup had never seen a rabbit, or any other game, in his life before. I once left a pup named Hector (now belonging to Mr. Ramsay, of Bray) hunting a hare or something, and, as I was in a hurry, I did not wait for him, but went on to Gomshall, a distance of four miles from home, thinking the pup would go home when he had lost me. But when I had just got to Gomshall, which was about one hour after, I heard him following full-cry ; so, after he had missed me, he got on my scent, and hunted me down, though I had crossed over ploughed fields, through very large woods, and through lanes, and on a track that I had never been before. The pup was only eight months old at the time. The same pup was out with Lord Burleigh's hounds on January 1st, 1881, when only seven months old, and I had the chance of putting him on the scent of a fox, to see if he would hunt him ; and he went off full-cry at once, although he had never seen a fox in his life. I have hunted deer with them ; but the proper game for them is the hare. They seem to hunt more offhand than the Foxhound and Harrier, and they give more music, and are keener than any English hound ; and although they have short legs, they get over the ground very fast—they take the scent so very easily, and don't seem to lose time in putting their heads up and down. I was once out with twelve of these hounds in a strange country to them, and they were hunting a rabbit or something ; but as I had no whipper-in, and as it was late in the afternoon, I wanted to get home, so I ran away from them, thinking that when they could not see me, and found that I had gone, they would leave off hunting rabbits. I ran about a mile across fields, towards home, and after the hounds had their hunt out, and could not find me, being in a part of the country they did not know, they immediately got on my track full cry. When I found what they were doing, I ran as fast as possible to have a good start, but they soon ran me down."

From the opinions and experiences quoted, it is evident that the Basset may be turned to account in many branches of sport ; and, notwithstanding some slight discrepancies in the statements, the whole speaks well for the utility of the breed. Only one more quotation on this head is needed, and it is from the article by Mr. Krehl in " Stonehenge's " book. " Deer and hares," says this eminently practical follower of the chase, " will actually play before the little hounds, stopping to listen to them coming." The games the deer and hares play on these agreeable occasions are, perhaps discreetly, not declared. There is no beast of chase that does not use its ears in endeavouring to escape, no matter what the nature of the pursuer.

I have already referred to Mr. Everett Millais' essay on " Bassets : their Use and Breeding," which he subsequently followed up with " Rational Breeding." Mr. Millais has collected a mass of facts, and has so marshalled them as to show, almost to a demonstration, the results certain to follow the mating of Bassets, in certain proportions of blood, of the strains of these hounds then possessed in England. The book is not an inviting one on first dipping into it, but well repays digestion. On first reading it, it will probably appear an enigma ; but a closer reading will disclose its sound common sense. The fact is, Mr. Millais has written for those who are supposed to know, and perfectly comprehend every allusion to, the types of hounds he speaks of ; but there he is in error : he should have defined his types, in order to make his arguments clear to the uninitiated in Basset mysteries.

In a correspondence Mr. Millais declared that " type cannot be defined more than fashion." " But fashion," replied Mr. Hugh

Dalziel, "can be defined; even a male creature, without being a milliner, can define and describe the difference between the type of ladies' head-gear that used to be called a 'cosy,' and that irreverently named the 'coal-scuttle,' up the long cavern of which those who would osculate had to venture as into a railway tunnel." Mr. Millais says: "Type is as changeable as fashion; were it not so, the Foxhound of to-day would be a very similar animal to what it was 100 years ago, which it is not." On the question of what constitutes type there is a great diversity of opinion. Mr. Millais preferred a Basset tricoloured, with tan head and black-and-white body; but that is not type: the type—that is to say, the generic characters—of the Basset, as of the Greyhound, was accurately, and with very considerable detail, described nearly 2,000 years ago, and remains essentially the same. As to our English hounds, the type has not been altered, but special developments, amounting merely to variations to meet altered methods of using the hounds, and the difference in the enjoyment sought to be derived from them, have been cultivated. Our Foxhounds of to-day were formed by selection 100 years ago, to meet new requirements, but the modifications made did not interfere with the essential character of them as hounds. Those only who set up imaginary types to suit their taste as fanciers, of whatever breed, imitate, and may, therefore, be compared to the rulers of fashion in dress and other trivialities.

Mr. Millais was, however, good enough to contribute to an earlier edition of this work his views of the three divisions of Bassets existing in England—namely, the Couteulx, or Fino de Paris; the Masson, or Termino; and the Lane—holding the term Couteulx Hound, as applied to all our Bassets, to be a most erroneous nomenclature. It is right, therefore, to present his views here, especially as they supply the great want in his essay, and should always be read, in conjunction with his remarks on breeding, by those interested in Bassets. Mr. Millais wrote:—

"When asked, some seven years ago, to write a small article on the Basset for 'British Dogs,' this hound could scarcely be called a British dog, the breed having only just begun to have a footing in England. Since then it has largely increased, and may now safely be classed as a British production.

Bassets may be classed in three divisions:—

1. Couteulx Hounds ...	...	...	}	Smooth-coated.
2. Lane Hounds	...	...		
3. Griffons ...	...	...	...	Rough-coated.

Of the first two varieties we have many examples at present; of the third, only one, to my knowledge, has been exhibited in England—namely, Ramoneau—though the type is common enough at Continental shows. To go into minute particulars of how the Basset has had its origin, or how it has thriven in this country, is not the object of these notes; though it will be necessary, in dealing with the Couteulx Hounds, to show how the two subdivisions, into which they must now be classed, have come about.

In the first place, before proceeding farther, it must be clearly understood what the terms 'Couteulx' and 'Lane' mean. When Bassets first began to be imported into England—I refer, of course, to our present stock, dating back to 1874—our hounds were imported from the kennels of Comte Couteulx le Cantalan, of Étrepagny. After a lapse of a few years a new kind of Basset made its appearance on the show-bench, exhibited by Mons. Louis Lane, of Francqueville, near Rouen.

So far, then, the terms 'Couteulx' and 'Lane' were applied to hounds emanating from the kennels of these two gentlemen. Fresh importations, however, arriving, and no new name occurring to breeders' minds for these hounds, the term 'Couteulx' has gradually come to mean any hound (smooth-coated) which is not a Lane, though, in truth, our smooth-coated Bassets might, with far greater advantages, be divided into the—

Couteulx	Fino de Paris type.
Masson	Termino type.
Lane	Ramono type.

I will, however, only speak of them as two varieties, the Couteulx and Lane; the former with two subdivisions.

COUTEULX HOUNDS

These hounds are exemplified by two types :—

    1. Fino de Paris type.
    2. Termino type.

Before proceeding to give the differences between the two types, it would be, perhaps, as well to understand how this has arisen. The following small pedigree table will show it :—

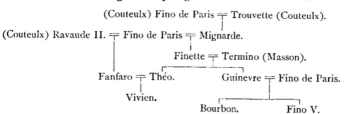

Although Guinevre and Théo were bred from Fino de Paris stock on the dam's side, they were of quite a different type from

Fino de Paris, or any other hound imported from Comte Couteulx's kennels; but they much resembled Bellicent, another of Mons. Masson's hounds imported into this country, which is a proof that this peculiar type is indigenous in his kennels. They must, therefore, have resembled their sire, which belonged to Mons. Masson. Bearing this well in mind, it is very easy to see how these two nearly related but different types have arisen.

On the importation of Guinevre, Théo, and Vivien into this country, the first-named bitch was mated with Fino de Paris. Had Guinevre followed the common rules of breeding, she should have given birth to pups of Fino de Paris type, but she did not; she chose to present one of them (Bourbon) in her own form, the type of Monsieur Masson's kennel, and that which I call the Termino type. The other pup, Fino V., resembled his sire, with the addition of some of his dam's quality.

Bourbon, being mated with his aunt, Théo, thus virtually breeding into the Masson or Termino side of the house, produced Chopette, a bitch excelling even her sire in points which make him so different from his Fino de Paris brother, Fino V.

In Vivien we have a bitch of very weak Termino type, so 'complaisant' as to throw both types whichever way mated, but who will throw her own, as in the case of Jupiter, a poor type-producer. In this way have arisen the two Couteulx types that we have at present on our show-benches.

FINO DE PARIS TYPE

Colour.—Rich tricolour—hare-pie, lemon, and white. The first object which strikes us is the brilliancy and general evenness of the markings: the tan is deep; the black, saddle-shaped on the back, running into tan on the buttocks.

Coat.—Thick, strong, and at times crimped even to coarseness; stern feathered.

Head.—In those unallied to the Termino hounds, flattish; ears set on high and small, but should be domed. In those containing Termino blood, the head is large, well shaped; ears hung low and of good size, with well-developed flews; nose slightly inclined to be Roman.

Eye.—Dark, sunken, and showing a prominent haw.

Bone.—Good; in those not too closely inbred, massive.

Legs.—Torses, demi-torses, droites.

General Appearance.—A fine large hound, of powerful physique.

Examples.—In the first instance, Fino de Paris as a type. In the second, Fino V., VI., Pallas II., Fresco, Forester, Merlin, Clovis, Eve, Texas Fino, Wazir, Aryan, Lælaps, Fancy, Fiddler, Flora.

TERMINO TYPE

Colour.—Tricolour (light), lemon-and-white, hare-pie, blue mottled. The tricolour of this hound is far less brilliant than in the preceding type, the tan being no longer so rich, whilst the black is distributed in uneven patches over the body, and, in addition to these markings, the hound is often "ticked," whilst frequently is to be seen a blue mottled appearance.

Coat.—Short and fine ; no crimping.
Head.—Domed, though in many of our best specimens this is not apparent.
Nose.—Strongly Roman, and finer than in the Fino de Paris hounds.
Ears.—Hung very low, and of immense length.
Flews.—Well marked.
Fye.—Dark, sunken, and hawed.
Bone.—Somewhat light, except in one or two specimens.
Legs.—Torses, demi-torses, droites, with an inclination to height.
General Appearance.—A fine, upstanding hound, well put together, and of high breeding.
Examples.—In the first instance, Termino (?), Guinevre, Bellicent. In the second degree, Bourbon, Chopette, Zeus, Beau, Beauclerc, Narcissus, Colinnette, Blondin, Dosia.

LANE HOUNDS

Colour.—Light tricolour, lemon-and-white, hare-pie (with ticking).
Coat.—Short, thick.
Head.—Should be domed ; somewhat large and coarse.
Ears.—Long, heavy, broad, and hung low.
Flews.—Well marked.
Eye.—Light.
Legs.—Torses.
Bone.—Enormous.
General Appearance.—A very big, heavy Basset ; coarse and clumsy, with enormous chest development.
Examples.—In the first instance, Ramono II. ; in the second instance, Gavotte, Blanchette II., Champion, Bavard, Chorister, Hannibal.

GRIFFONS

Colour.—Tricolour, blue-grey, hare-pie, lemon-and-white.
Coat.—Thick, hard, wire-haired, and like that of the Otter-hound.
Head.—Such as that of the Otter-hound, and well flewed.
Eye.—Dark and hawed.
Ears.—Long and pendulous, low hung.
Bone.—Good.
Legs.—Torses.
General Appearance.—A strong, active hound, powerful, and well knit together.
Example.—Ramoneau."

Readers of the foregoing interesting contribution, will readily see that type and fashion could each be defined ; for in his article Mr. Millais has described not merely one type of Basset, but (including the broken-haired Griffon) four, and has thereby proved that he had estimated his own ability too modestly. Perhaps the term " type " is too strong to apply to the slight variations described, which, in fact, amount merely to small differences in features, always showing variations in families. We would say of the Scottish Highlanders, they are of Celtic type ; but the term would not be used to describe some minute difference that may have been observable between the Clan Macgregor and the Clan Macdonald. It is, however, the order of the day, in regard to dogs, to sub-divide with such great minuteness that it is only given to those inspired with the peculiar afflatus of "the fancy" to appreciate every microscopic difference dealt with.

It has frequently been urged that the points of a dog, of whatever breed, must, if worthy of appreciation, be capable of demonstration in terms comprehensible to every one. Mr. Millais was certainly not one of those who cannot express in language the differences they distinguish in the animals they judge; and it will be acknowledged that he did good service in plainly stating the distinguishing features of the four varieties of Basset-hounds as they were types fixed in his mind. It is a decided advantage to have the points, or, as the old school of breeders called them, "the properties," of each breed defined. If the definition proves to be wrong, or capable of amendment in any way, it can be done; but without a written definition we are left to the incompetence of egotists, who claim to be inspired, and able to see a something they call " character," indefinable by them, and invisible to all but themselves and the privileged few initiated in the mystery.

Though it is not difficult to accept Mr. Millais' distinction between the Fino de Paris and the Termino Hounds, the same can hardly be said of his theory of breeding, which appears to rest on an insufficiently solid basis, leaving out of account influences which sometimes assert themselves in a way to all of us inexplicable.

Fino de Paris was bred from brother and sister—farther than his grandparents his pedigree is unknown. Termino is said, as a sire, to show more prepotency, stamping the character of his family against odds in favour of Fino de Paris; yet the pedigree of Termino is unknown. To square results, in this case, with the accumulated experiences of breeders, Termino's pedigree, although unwritten, must be the longest, and most free from foreign admixture.

The facts of the case appear to be that Comte Couteulx and MM. Masson and Lane have each bred his own strain from the same common stock. It is, therefore, going too far to base a system on present results in England of any combinations of these strains, until several more generations of breeding from existing results are seen.

Most of the above has already appeared in earlier editions of this work, but it is of so much interest to present-day breeders that it has been deemed worthy of repetition. Since the above remarks were penned, the Basset has increased enormously in popularity, both in the field and on the show-bench. Among the successful breeders have been, in addition to those already mentioned, Mrs. C. C. Ellis, who produced a remarkable succession of champions from her kennels, Mrs. Walsh, Mrs. Tottie, Mr. Harry Jones, Mr. F. B. Craven, Mr. G. T. G. Musson, Dr. S. Isaacke, Mr. W. W. White, Major Owen Swaffield, Mr. McNeill, Captain

Stone, Mr. G. Dalton, Mr. B. F. Parrott, the Messrs. Heseltine, Mrs. A. N. Lubbock, Miss Wimbush, Mr. C. Garnett, Captain Crowe, Dr. Woodhead, Mr. Roberts, Mr. J. Stark, Mr. C. R. Morrison, Mr. Lord, Prince Pless, Hon. C. B. Courtenay, Mr. Kenyon Fuller, Mr. A. Croxton Smith, and many others. The King and Queen are acknowledged lovers of the showy little hound, and good specimens, mainly bred at Sandringham, are from time to time exhibited by them.

Quite a number of packs, too, exist for the purpose of hare-hunting, and it is pleasing to find that in the majority of instances Masters are breeding to type. One or two attempts have been made to produce a longer legged hound, but the idea has not met with favour, and most Basset-hound men of to-day will be thoroughly in sympathy with the concluding remarks of Mr. Blain, quoted on a previous page.

Below we give the points and description of the Basset-hound, originally drawn up by Mr. G. R. Krehl, and accepted at a club meeting in 1899 :—

POINTS OF THE BASSET-HOUND (SMOOTH)

	VALUE.
Head, Skull, Eyes, Muzzle, and Flews	15
Ears	15
Neck, Dewlap, Chest, and Shoulders	10
Fore Legs and Feet	15
Back, Loins, and Hindquarters	10
Stern	5
Coat and Skin	10
Colour and Markings	15
"Basset Character" and Symmetry	5
Total	100

GENERAL APPEARANCE

1. To begin with the *Head*, as the most distinguishing part of all breeds. The head of the Basset-hound is most perfect when it closest resembles a Blood-hound's. It is long and narrow, with heavy flews, occiput prominent, "*la bosse de la chasse*," and forehead wrinkled to the eyes, which should be kind, and show the haw. The general appearance of the head must present high breeding and reposeful dignity; the teeth are small, and the upper jaw sometimes protrudes. This is not a fault, and is called the "*bec de lièvre.*"

2. The *Ears* very long, and when drawn forward folding well over the nose— so long that in hunting they will often actually tread on them ; they are set on low, and hang loose in folds like drapery, the ends inward curling, in texture thin and velvety.

3. The *Neck* is powerful, with heavy dewlaps. Elbows must not turn out. The chest is deep, full, and framed like a "man-of-war." Body long and low.

4. *Fore Legs* short, about 4in., and close-fitting to the chest till the crooked knee, from where the wrinkled ankle ends in a massive paw, each toe standing out distinctly.

5. The *Stifles* are bent, and the quarters full of muscle, which stands out so

that when one looks at the dog from behind, it gives him a round, barrel-like effect. This, with their peculiar, waddling gait, goes a long way towards Basset character—a quality easily recognised by the judge, and as desirable as Terrier character in a Terrier.

6. The *Stern* is coarse underneath, and carried hound-fashion.

7. The *Coat* is short, smooth, and fine, and has a gloss on it like that of a racehorse. (To get this appearance, they should be hound-gloved, never brushed.) Skin loose and elastic.

8. The *Colour* should be black, white, and tan ; the head, shoulders, and quarters a rich tan, and black patches on the back. They are also sometimes hare-pied.

POINTS OF THE BASSET-HOUND (ROUGH)

	Value.
Head and Ears	... 20
Body, including Hindquarters	... 35
Legs and Feet	... 20
Coat	... 15
" Basset Character," etc.	... 10
Total	... 100

GENERAL APPEARANCE

1. The *Head* should be large, the skull narrow but of good length, the peak well-developed. The muzzle should be strong, and the jaws long and powerful ; a snipy muzzle and weakness of jaw are objectionable. The eyes should be dark and not prominent. The ears should be set on low, of good length and fine texture.

2. The *Neck* should be strong, of good length and muscular, set on sloping shoulders.

3. The *Body* should be massive, of good length, and well ribbed up, any weakness or slackness of loin being a bad fault. The chest should be large and very deep, the sternum prominent.

4. The *Fore Legs* should be short and very powerful, very heavy in bone, either half crooked or nearly straight. The elbows should lie against the side of the chest, and should not turn out.

5. *Hindquarters* should be powerful and muscular ; the hind legs should be rather longer than the fore legs, and should be well bent at the stifles.

6. *Stern.*—Of moderate length and carried gaily ; should be set on high.

7. *Coat.*—An extremely important point. It should be profuse, thick and harsh to the touch, with a dense undercoat. The coat may be wavy.

8. *Colour.*—Any recognised hound colour.

9. *Weight.*—Dogs from 40lb. to 50lb., bitches rather less.

The Rough Basset should appear a very powerful hound for his size, on short, strong legs. Body massive and good length, without slackness of loin. The feet should be thick, well padded, and not open. The expression should be kindly and intelligent. Any unsoundness should disqualify the hound.

Of recent years an emphatic stand has been made against unsoundness, and hounds that at one time would have won prizes on account of their beautiful type would now be sent out of the ring unnoticed. This is quite the right line to go upon, for the

Basset is essentially a sporting hound, and every effort should be made to breed out unsound front legs or weak loins and quarters. Though many people keep Bassets simply for show purposes or as pets, there is no reason why the working properties should occupy a secondary position in the esteem of the breeder. Indeed, the writer would almost prefer seeing a sporting breed become extinct than suffer the degradation of being propagated simply for so-called "fancy" points. We should try for a well-balanced hound, beautiful in head, with the pathetic expression which is so much of his charm, short legs, with feet beyond reproach, well-sprung ribs, and deep chest. Why some people should wish for longer legs it

FIG. 53.—MRS. TOTTIE'S SMOOTH BASSET-HOUND CHAMPION LOUIS LE BEAU.

is difficult to imagine. The Basset was never meant for speed, and, rather than take away one of his chief characteristics, those who want a faster pack should take up Beagles instead. The note of the little hound is deep and melodious.

As with so many other varieties, persistent inbreeding for the maintenance of type has resulted in a greater susceptibility to distemper. In order to strengthen the constitution and also get an increase in size, the late Sir Everett Millais made experiments in the direction of a Bloodhound cross, and the results in the third generation were certainly striking. For some reason or other, however, breeders did not lend a ready favour to the idea, and no one has followed it up. As a rule, sensational figures are not paid for Bassets, and quite a little excitement was caused at Cruft's

Show in 1900 when Mrs. Tottie claimed Mr. A. Croxton Smith's Wantage for the catalogue price of £150. At an earlier day Mr. Krehl obtained a somewhat similar sum. The illustrations (Fig. 53 and 54) show the present-day type of hound.

Bassets vary a good deal in disposition. Some make delightful companions, becoming much attached to master or mistress, while others display a stubbornness which requires considerable humouring. On the whole, it is mainly a question of early training.

FIG. 54.—SMOOTH BASSET-HOUND CHAMPION XENA. BRED BY
MRS. C. C. ELLIS.

In choosing a puppy, select one with plenty of bone and substance. See that the ears are set on low and fold gracefully, instead of hanging flat to the side of the skull. Beware, too, of those with very narrow heads—they are likely to become snipy. The skin should be loose and fine to the touch, and the eyes should be deep set and show some haw, as with the Bloodhound. The legs should be clean at the shoulder, without any tendency to bow out : the writer prefers them wrinkled down to the feet, which should be large and clumsy-looking for the size of the puppy,

CLOSELY allied as it is to the Dachshund, the Basset Hound is, thanks both to the popularity of the former breed and the energy of its own admirers, beginning to take a firm root on English soil. Mr. Everett Millais, of Palace Gate, South Kensington, London, is an enthusiastic admirer of the variety, and has spared neither time nor money in his endeavours to do it justice. As he has kindly provided us with some valuable and practical information on the breed, we think it desirable that his remarks should appear in the earlier portions of the article, as he not only alludes to the introduction of the Basset Hound to the show bench of this country, but also supplements his remarks with dates :—

"That the Basset Français and the German Dachshund or Basset Allemand were originally from common ancestors I am not going to deny, but that the Basset Français has preserved more especially his individuality is undoubted ; inasmuch as while the Basset Français, a hound in every sense of the word, reproduces specimens of his own type, the Basset Allemand, or German Dachshund, gives birth to puppies of a hound and also a terrier type in the same litter. Of course this shows the infusion of foreign blood at some period or other, which I hope soon to see eradicated.

"That these two different breeds of Bassets are now quite distinct I am sure of. One has only to visit the Jardin d'Acclimatation to see them exhibited as such. In corroboration of my statement I quote a letter by that eminent French author, Mons. A. Pierre Pichot, editor of *La Revue Britannique*, member of the committees on French dog shows, and one of the directors of the Jardin d'Acclimatation :—

"'*To the Editor of the "Live Stock Journal."*'

"'The Basset Hounds, which differ in almost every point from the Dachshund, are, on the contrary, of every colour and both rough and smooth, and of these there are still more numerous varieties than of the Dachshund, the Bassets having in my own opinion sprung from the different local breeds of large hounds, and therefore connected with the Vendée, Saintonge, Artois, and Normandy types.

"'*December 3rd, 1875.*'

"I may here mention that the only Bassets yet exhibited in England have been of the Normandy type, *à poil*, and one of the Vendée type, a Basset Griffon. I have only lately received a letter from a gentleman in Wales who informs me that he has imported a leash of the latter hounds for rabbiting, and so I now hope to see an increase of them, as the only one I mention above is a dog belonging to Mr. de Landre Macdona—a very fine specimen, but deficient in leather.

"Concerning the first introduction of the breed into this country, my mind goes back to the Wolverhampton Dog Show, 1875, where my first Basset Français was to make his *début*. On my arrival I was directed to the Talbot Hotel, as being nearest to the Agricultural Hall. It was late when I got back to the hotel, after seeing my hound chained up under his appointed number, and having dined I descended to the smoking-room, where several gentlemen were taking their ease, and anarchy in the shape of dog-talk presided.

"One of the gentlemen commenced to talk to me, and the following remarks took place :—

" ' Showing Terriers ? ' said one.

" ' Bulls ? ' said another.

" ' No,' I replied, ' a Basset.'

" ' A what ? '

" ' A Basset,' I repeated.

" ' What's he like,' said another, winking at the gentleman who sat next him.

" ' Oh, he's about 4 feet long and 12 inches high.'

"At this announcement there was a general desire to see the wonderful animal. I replied that I had already taken him to the show, but that I would be only too delighted to show him to them in the morning.

" I merely mention this to prove that even the breed of the dog had scarcely reached the ears of those whose duties led them, before other people, in the way of hearing it.

" Great was the excitement that day in the canine world when the hound was led into the ring, and at night many were the cups emptied by those who had seen the breed often before, but couldn't exactly remember where.

" Amongst Dachshund fanciers the sensation he caused may be gathered from the various letters which appeared shortly after the Wolverhampton show, wherein my hound, weighing then between 50 and 60 lbs., was pronounced by Dachshund fanciers, from a reported description, to be an overgrown specimen of their particular hobby.

" These letters produced no results as to clearing up the doubts, so I determined to exhibit at the forthcoming Crystal Palace show not only my Basset Français, but also a Dachshund. With the Dachshund I got highly commended, and with the Basset Français first in the variety class. The following were the remarks on the hound by the *Live Stock Journal* after the show :—

" ' Mr. Everett Millais's Model was likewise amongst the winners (foreign class). This exquisitely pretty little hound was greatly admired, and acknowledged by Dachshund fanciers to be a totally distinct variety.'

" It was here that the Earl of Onslow, now the largest proprietor of these hounds, first saw a Basset Français. Struck by the singular beauty of the hound (which is a rich tricolour) he procured a pair from France. These, however, being aged, he again procured a couple and a half from Comte Couteul (1876), viz., Fino, Nestor, and Finette. All these hounds are of the Normandy type.

" This year (1880) at the Crystal Palace the Basset Français class was entirely composed of the above type, either imported or bred from imported parents, with the exception of two, one of which was Mr. Macdona's Basset Griffon (Vendée type) which I have mentioned before, and the other a tricoloured nondescript; the Normandy type of hounds belonging to Lord Onslow and myself.

" As in Germany anything with crooked legs is called a Dachshund, so in France for the same reason 'the anything' is called a Chien Basset, for the simple reason that people do not know better. In England it is the same ; the word Terrier is good enough for the whole race, whether pure or mongrel. The other day I smiled on hearing men, who ought to know better, describe a well-known Skye Terrier breeder's team in the Park as Dandie Dinmont pups !

"The word 'Basset' is such a large word, that to ask a French sportsman for a Basset would be precisely as putting the same question to him, substituting the word 'horse' for 'Basset.' You might want a cart-horse, a cob, a hack, a racehorse, &c.

"In like manner there are various breeds of Bassets.

"The word 'Basset,' which means a 'dwarf dog,' is applied to all short and crooked-legged dogs, and those which appear to have had an accident in their puppyhood.

"I know many authors put this defect down to rickets, but I believe that these animals have been, like the mole, provided by Nature to do a certain work, which could not be done by those on high and straight limbs.

"Bassets are divided into two distinct breeds—the Basset Français and the Basset Allemand, which is the German Dachshund. So let us put this latter aside without further ado.

"Now the Bassets Français are divided into two classes—the *Basset à poil ras* (smooth-coated), and the *Basset à poil dur*, more commonly known as the 'Basset Griffon.'

"Both the smooth-coated and the rough-coated varieties are divided into three classes, and are named after the crookedness, if one may so express it, of their fore-paws. The names are as follows :—The crooked-legged (*Basset à jambes torses*); the half crooked-legged (*Basset à jambes demi-torses*); the straight-legged (*Basset à jambes droites*).

"So as to make my readers more easily able to distinguish the difference between the *Basset à jambes torses* and the *Basset à jambes droites*, more frequently known as the 'petit chien courant,' let me refer them to the two engravings, reproduced from a well-known French book on dogs used for sport, 'Chiens de Chasse.'

"The first engraving is that of the heavy *Basset à jambes torses*. Mark the high conical head, heavy flews, pendulous ears, and deep-set eyes. There is but one mistake in this drawing, and that is that the chest is not properly developed. It should come down straight to the ankle joints. A small ball may be observed, attached to the hinder hound's neck. This is a 'grelot,' and is put on for the purpose of letting the sportsman know where his hound is when in cover, but not on game.

"The second engraving is that of a couple of *Bassets à jambes droites*. The reader will see at once that the flews have disappeared, and that the hound is of a much lighter build than the *Basset à jambes torses*.

"Now the variety of these names is very confusing, and for sporting purposes the intending purchaser must exercise his own judgment when making a purchase. Should his ground be flat and easy to get over, then by all means have the long, low, heavy hound with crooked legs ; but should it be of a stony and marshy description, with deep cuttings, &c., then one of the two latter. The rough-coated hounds are of course used for what might be called the hard work.

"The Basset, for its size, has more bone, perhaps, than nearly any other dog.

"The skull should be peaked like that of the Bloodhound, with the same dignity and expression, nose black (although some of my own have white about theirs), and well flewed. For the size of the hound, I think the teeth are extremely small. However, as they are not intended to destroy life, this is probably the reason.

"The ears should hang like the Bloodhound's, and are like the softest velvet drapery.

"The eyes are a deep brown, and are brimful of affection and intelligence. They are pretty deeply set, and should show a considerable haw. A Basset is one of those hounds incapable of having a wicked eye.

"The neck is long, but of great power ; and in the *Basset à jambes torses* the flews extend very nearly down to the chest. The chest is more expansive in the Basset than even in the Bulldog, and should in the *Bassets à jambes torses* be not more than two inches from the ground. In the case of the *Basset à jambes demi-torses* and *jambes droites*, being generally lighter, their chests do not, of course, come so low.

"The shoulders are of great power, and terminate in the crooked feet of the Basset, which appear to be a mass of joints. The back and ribs are strong, and the former of great length. The stern is gaily carried like that of hounds in general, and when the hound is on the scent of game this portion of his body gets extremely animated, and tell me, in my own hounds, when they have struck a fresh or cold scent, and I even know when the foremost hound will give tongue.

· "The hind-quarters are very strong and muscular, the muscles standing rigidly out down to the hocks.

"The skin is soft in the smooth-haired dogs, and like that of any other hound, but in the rough variety it is identical with that of the Otter-hound's.

"Colour, of course, is a matter of fancy, although I infinitely prefer the 'tricolour,' which has a tan head and black-and-white body.

"The Griffons generally are like the Otter-hounds in colouring.

"As to points, in a breed like this it is impossible, unless one had a class for every division. I hope, however, to see at the Kennel Show a class for the Basset Griffon, as well as for those of the *poil ras*.

"Bassets are used for tracking boar, wolves, deer, and turning them out of the woods and copses. They are likewise used for pheasant and general sporting purposes, where game is scarce. To use them in this country would be impossible, but I have done so in Scotland on the hill-sides, where avenues had been cut in the bracken, and very good sport was the result. Their affection is wonderful to their owner, but strangers they dislike. Their memory is wonderful. When at Lowestoft a friend, who lived in the next house, pushed my old dog from the door-step one day, to come in. Model deeply resented this, and never would allow 'that friend' in without growling, and turning up his bristles like a clothes-brush.

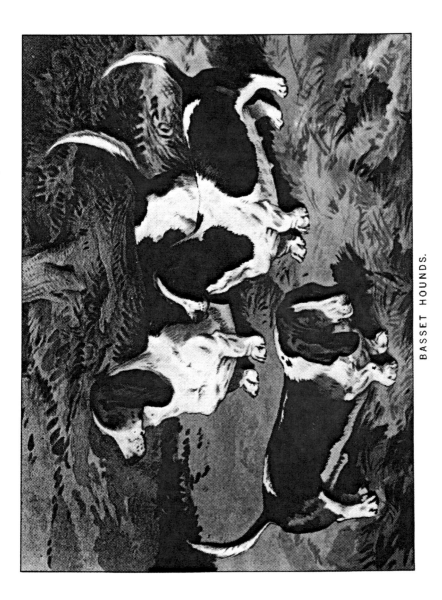

BASSET HOUNDS.

"I run mine as Beagles, and many people who have been with them infinitely prefer the sport, as they never run over a scent, and the pace, though a hard trot, is not too fast.

"Comte Couteul, from whom Lord Onslow and I got mine, writes the following in his book, 'History of the French Hounds' :—

"'These Bassets have never been well known in England, though an eminent writer asserts to the contrary. It is only within the last four or five years that they have been spoken of as hounds for hunting, and even now they are very scarce in Great Britain.

"'At the first French dog show in Paris, 1863, many English visitors expressed their astonishment at this type of dog, which was so new to them, though the same general outline is reproduced in the Clumber and Turnspit breeds. In fact, though at the present time several English

BASSET À JAMBES DROITES.

sportsmen may have in their possession some French Bassets or German Dachshunds (this kind being much used in Germany for hunting the badger), it may be said that these hounds are as new to the English "veneur" as our own existing packs of Gascony and Saintonge hounds.'

"The Count further goes on to state that the reason of this is the absurd and selfish way that French masters of hounds have (up to the time of his writing) kept secret the fruits of their experience, or, as the Count himself describes it, 'hide their hounds like stolen treasures.'

Mr. Everett Millais having entered so thoroughly upon the subject of Basset Hounds, and being the recognised authority on the breed at present in the country, a very few lines from us will suffice to close the chapter referring to this class of dog. From the remarks of Mr. Millais few can doubt the high qualifications of the Basset for recognition as both a sporting and companionable dog, and from what we have learnt concerning him from other sources, we have no doubt but that his good character is a thoroughly well-deserved one. In appearance he is more showy than his relative the Dachshund, though it must be admitted against him that his greater size renders him a trifle less desirable as an indoor pet.

We can thoroughly endorse the above remarks concerning the affection of the Basset towards his master, and are convinced that there is a great future of popularity in store for this very engaging breed.

There is, however, almost the same difficulty before the Basset as a show dog, as there is in the case of his relative the Dachshund. We refer to the *two types*, the existence of which will always breed dissensions amongst exhibitors, unless one class is provided for Bassets à jambes torses, and another for Bassets à jambes droites. Believers in one type will find it very trying to be beaten by a dog of the (to them) distasteful shape, and may be disheartened,

MR. EVERETT MILLAIS'S BASSET HOUND "MODEL."

and therefore possibly retire from exhibiting in future. However, a defeat under such circumstances is not so serious a matter as it would be in the Dachshund classes, where many of the supporters of one type maintain that their dogs are the *only* true representatives of the breed, and specimens varying materially from them are mongrels. Amongst Basset breeders the existence of the two types is recognised; and though a preference may be shown for one of them by any breeder, he must bear in mind that his neighbour's dogs, though differing from his own in formation, may be equally pure Basset Hounds.

The illustration, by Mr. C. B. Barber, of Mr. Millais's splendid specimen Model, is, in our opinion, an exact representation of that well-known dog, whose name will never cease to be associated with the introduction of the breed into this country.

Model has won the following prizes amongst others: Twice first Crystal Palace, first Brighton, second Alexandra Palace, second Agricultural Hall, and third Darlington. Such performances, taking into consideration that he had to be shown in variety classes against dogs of all sorts of breeds, stamps Model as a remarkably successful competitor in the ring.

We append a table of weights and measurements of Mr. Everett Millais's Bassets, Model and Garenne, which he has kindly sent us for insertion.

	MODEL.	GARENNE.
Age	7½ yrs.	2½ yrs.
Weight	46 lbs.	28 lbs.
Height at shoulder	12 inches.	9½ inches.
Length from nose to set on of tail	32 ,,	29 ,,
,, of tail	11½ ,,	9 ,,
Girth of chest	25 ,,	20 ,,
,, of loin	21 ,,	16 ,,
,, of head	17 ,,	13 ,,
,, of fore-arm	6½ ,,	5 ,,
Length of head from occiput to tip of nose	9 ,,	8 ,,
Girth of muzzle midway between eyes and tip of nose	9½ ,,	7 ,,
Length of ears from tip to tip	19 ,,	17 ,,
Height from ground, fore-feet	2¾ ,,	2½ ,,

As regards a scale of points for judging Bassets, we are of opinion that the scale given in the preceding chapter on Dachshunds can be used with good results, and therefore refer our readers to that instead of repeating it here.

"IT is surprising how soon a want of care, or care wrongly directed, leads to the degeneracy of a domestic race." Thus speaks Mr. Darwin in his "Descent of Man," and no practical breeder of any sort of stock can be found to disagree with him. No care and attention on the part of the owner and his servants can turn a badly-bred, ill-formed animal into a good one; and though it is impossible to bestow too much consideration on the treatment of the stock, all exertions on behalf of animals badly bred will be, as a rule, thrown away when they come before the judge. Years of anxiety go for nothing, if due attention is not paid not only to the health and strength, but also to the proper selection of the breeding stock. As in the articles on the various breeds full prominence has been given to the special points which must be studied in each individual variety, it is unnecessary here for us to go beyond a general outline of the management of what may be called the breeding materials.

It is wonderful to reflect upon the success which seems to attend the efforts of some of the most loosely-conducted establishments, and to see winner after winner turned out from a kennel where no rules of breeding are for a moment studied, and where the management is often left by the owner in the hands of a kennel-man whose knowledge of the breed is absolutely *nil*. Such success in the few instances in which it occurs is eventually unfortunate in its results, both to the breeders of the dogs themselves and also to many of the outside world, who, either to save themselves trouble, or through ignorance of the simplest principles of breeding, ignorantly rush for the services of the nearest prize-winner, utterly regardless as to whether he is likely to "nick" with the bitch they propose uniting with him, in shape, size, or pedigree. The result may be a temporary success, but is certain ultimate destruction of all type. Breeding *can* be regulated by rules and judicious selection, else how do we see so many breeds of dogs now in existence (which we can prove to have originated from a cross of two older varieties) keep on throwing puppies which consistently resemble their parents in every property, and whose difference from them only consists in minor insignificant and immaterial features? By rigidly adhering to an ideal type, and resisting all temptations to go from it, a breeder is certain in time to find himself in possession of the sort of dog he has, rightly or wrongly, determined on possessing; and then he is in a position to discover, from the success of his dogs, whether his exertions are to be repaid or not.

We must commence, then, by impressing upon all beginners, and many older hands, the desirability of adhering to *one type* if they want to make a name for themselves as amateur breeders. Of course, in the case of those who breed solely for the market it is right that they should produce good specimens of every recognised standard, so as to please buyers, whatever their own opinions may be; but as these remarks are not intended to be addressed to dealers, who are perfectly competent to manage their own business, but to amateurs, it is sufficient to point out the importance of adhering to one type. By breeding to one standard, we necessarily imply that no one should be induced to set up as a producer of canine stock until he has clearly made up his mind what sort of animal he wishes for. In the case of a beginner, there is generally an acquaintance at hand who possesses more or less experience in such matters, and who, if he be a real lover of the dog, will be glad to place his services at his young friend's disposal. The opinions of such an individual may not all be correct; but if he be fairly competent, and honest, he can always be useful to the beginner. It is a great assistance, too, in arriving at a correct opinion, if the uses for which the various breeds have been brought into existence are brought under consideration. It is no good breeding a dog, though he be ever so handsome-looking, if he is palpably unfit for the work he is supposed to perform if called upon ; and, under a judge who knows his work, a flashy-looking dog often has to lower his colours to his more sober and workman-like neighbour, whose undoubted good properties have escaped the attention of the uninitiated.

Having decided upon the type which he himself desires to produce, a beginner should make it his next business to ascertain if his ideas in any way resemble the orthodox standard ; if so, his labours are considerably diminished, as his object in breeding will be to obtain the services of such stud dogs as he particularly admires, and in whose pedigree he has satisfied himself there is no bar sinister. It is an indisputable fact that a well-bred dog is far more likely to beget stock resembling himself than a good-looking mongrel is. Again, in the case of the former, even if he fails to impress his own likeness on his progeny, there is a possibility, if not a fair amount of certainty, that the puppies will throw back to a well-bred ancestor of more or less elegant proportions ; whilst with a dog whose pedigree is enveloped in mystery or something worse, there is a chance of the young ones displaying every conceivable type and temper.

The subject of in-breeding is one which has exercised the minds of breeders for many a day, and affords matter for a controversy which seems far from being brought to a termination. There can be no sort of doubt that, if carried to too great a length, in-breeding stunts the growth and weakens the intelligence and constitution of all dogs. This opinion is, we believe, unanimously received by all breeders of canine stock; though, in the case of game-cocks more than one authority has it that incestuously-bred birds are stouter, gamer, and more active than those whose parents are unrelated to each other. Observation has proved that the union of father with daughter and mother with son is far preferable, where dogs are concerned, to an alliance between brother and sister. Once in and twice out is, we believe, an excellent system if the crosses are judiciously selected, and the reasons for this appear to be as follows :— A breeder has a dog belonging to a strain which usually produces good-headed ones, but apt to be leggy and perhaps deficient in coat. He naturally wishes to remedy these defects, and in many instances selects as a mate a dog indifferent in head, but good in bone and in jacket; the result being most probably one fair puppy and several very indifferent ones which inherit the faults of both their sire and dam. On the other hand, however, had he exercised a little patience, and mated his dog with one of the same strain, thereby strengthening the probability of the puppies being in their turn likely to beget good-headed offspring when allied with another strain of blood, he would, in the course of a few years, have most probably got exactly the sort of dog he desired to obtain. We are perfectly aware that this argument may be said to cut both ways, and that those taking a contrary view of the case to our own may exclaim that the faults are just as likely to be perpetuated as the good properties; but we would observe that perpetual wandering from one blood to another *must* eventually produce specimens of uncertain type, whose services at the stud are perfectly useless from the fact that there is no fixed character in their breeding, and who are liable to throw puppies of every conceivable shape and make in the same litter. In short, in-breeding is, when judiciously carried out, absolutely essential to a breeder's success as a breeder, if such is to be maintained.

Finally, before closing our remarks upon the general subject of breeding, we wish to warn beginners that they are undertaking a tedious and very disappointing pursuit when they set up to be breeders of exhibition dogs. The best of calculations are often upset by accident or fate, and many a promising puppy falls a victim to the ills that puppyhood is peculiarly heir to. To have bred a first-rate dog of any breed is indeed a thing to be proud of, when it is considered how many scores of persons are expending time and money and judgment upon this very object. How few champions there are in the world is a statement which can be read in two ways—either there are so few that it should be an easy matter to add to their number; or it may be construed as implying that a vast amount of labour is wasted in trying to produce what is in reality a matter of chance. To us there appears to be both truth and untruth in each opinion; but the fact remains that champions have arisen, and will arise again, and are far more likely to be brought into existence when due attention is paid to the mates a breeder selects for his dogs.

Careful people invariably keep regular stud books referring to their breeding operations; in these the date of birth (and if necessary of the purchase), colour, sex, weight, breeder, and performances of their stock, are registered. The visits of their own bitches, and of others to their stud dogs, are also entered; as are the dates of sales, and the names and addresses of the purchasers. By this means ready and accurate information can be obtained concerning the history of any animal which may at one time or other pass through their hands.

THE STUD DOG.

A great deal of a breeder's success depends upon the state of health in which the stud dog is when he begets offspring; for a delicate or unhealthy dog is more than likely to transmit his defects to his puppies, who are in consequence more difficult to rear, and of less value when they attain maturity. Considerable attention should therefore be paid to the comfort of a dog who is in the habit of receiving a large number of stud visits. He should, if possible, be well exercised morning and evening, either by a country walk, or a run round his owner's yard; and his diet must be wholesome and liberal. A plunge in cold water materially assists in keeping a dog in vigorous condition, and in warm weather may be taken daily. It should be borne in mind, too, that it is always well to have your stud dogs look clean and tidy, both when out of doors and when in the kennels. Much depends upon the first impressions formed by the owner of a bitch who contemplates breeding from him, and many a dog is passed over whose services, had he been in better fettle, might have been resorted to. Care should be taken not to overtax the energies of a young sire by allowing him to receive too many stud visits; the result of excesses in this way being both sickly offspring and his own ultimate failure at the stud. Fifteen or twenty bitches a year are quite enough for a dog not in his prime, and about twice the number for a dog in the full vigour of his strength. As a rule, dogs under eighteen months old are not likely to do themselves or their owners much good if bred from; and availing one's self of the services of a very old dog is always risky. It is extremely hard to state an age at which a dog can be said to be "old"; some retain the vigour of their youth up to ten years and more, whilst others get decrepit and break up at six or seven. So much depends upon constitution and careful attendance, that it is impossible to advise upon the age at which a stud dog ceases to be of use; but breeders should see the dog for themselves, if they do not know him, and judge, from his appearance and condition, whether he is likely to suit their wishes.

On the arrival of a bitch for service, the owner of the stud dog should, unless time is a matter of consideration, fasten her up securely, and let her recover from the fatigues of her journey before the introduction takes place. A night's rest and a feed are very likely to assist nature's course, a bitch served immediately after a tiring journey being far more likely to miss conception than one who has rested and become a little accustomed to the place and those around her. Many bitches are very troublesome and restive when with the dog, and throw themselves about in a most violent manner; others are savage and morose, and if not carefully looked after are likely to fly at him and perhaps do some serious injury. In such cases the bitch must be held by the collar, but care should be taken that she does not get half suffocated by too tight a grasp being placed on it. The possibility of a fight taking place, or of the dog requiring some assistance, especially in the case of young bitches, make it undesirable that the pair should be left alone together for any length of time, much less after connection is terminated.

After union it is some time before the animals can be separated : twenty minutes is about the average, though, of course, this period is often exceeded or decreased in duration. After that the breeder must wait patiently for Nature to take its course, when the bitch should be kenneled by herself on straw, and kept as quiet as possible. It is desirable that a second visit should, if possible, be paid after an interval of thirty-six or forty-eight hours. The majority of the owners of stud dogs gladly consent to this arrangement, as it lessens the chances of the bitch proving barren, and also saves them trouble, and their dog from getting a bad name as a stock-getter.

A sire should be looked upon with suspicion if his services are in too great request, and the number of his receptions unlimited, as it is only reasonable to expect sickly offspring from a dog whose stud experiences are practically unrestricted. A very old dog, unless mated to a young and vigorous bitch, is more than likely to fail to beget stock at all : and if he succeeds in doing so, the puppies are very frequently of bad constitution and delicate in their earlier days. It is often the case that the services of a successful show dog are most eagerly sought after by breeders, and the merits of his *father* entirely overlooked ; and this is certainly a fact which must puzzle all practical men when they reflect upon it. A sire of good pedigree, who can produce stock of superior quality to himself, is better worth patronising at a low fee than his successful son who has yet to prove himself the success at the stud which he is on the bench or in the field ; especially as in the latter instance the sum charged for his services is sure to be a considerable one. Many of our champion dogs have turned out complete failures from a breeder's point of view ; whilst their plainer-looking fathers or brothers have begotten offspring of a far better stamp, though with only half the chances of success. A golden rule in dog-breeding is, for the owner to satisfy himself that his bitch *really does* visit the dog he has selected for her. In many instances we know tricks to have been played upon owners who have sent their bitches to dogs at a distance ; and we have ourselves been applied to for the services of a dog, standing at a low fee, by an owner of a stud dog, for a bitch sent up to the latter. Unfortunately, in ignorance of the fact, we granted his request, and only afterwards discovered what had occurred, and that the bitch, the name of whose owner we never ascertained, had been sent up to this gentleman's dog, and was not one of his own. The difference between the fees of the two dogs was three guineas ; and as it was impossible for us to *prove* that the owner was not informed of what took place, we were unable to take steps in the matter, and our acquaintance still walks the streets an honest man. If the distance is too far to accompany the bitch or send one's man, it is a very good plan to get a friend in the neighbourhood of the stud dog's kennel to accompany her when she visits him, especially in dealing with strangers. Of course, in the case of owners whose characters are above suspicion these precautions are unnecessary ; but it will always be a satisfaction to the proprietor of a stud dog to know that the bitch's visit has been witnessed by her owner or his nominee, especially if she should fail to be in pup. In event of the latter being the case, the usual practice is that the same bitch may visit the dog a second time gratuitously, or another of the same owner's at half price ; but here again caution must be exercised on the part of the proprietor of the stud dog, for instances have occurred when puppies have been born dead, and he has been told there was no result from the union of the parents. Owners of stud dogs often do, and always should, provide the owners of bitches which have visited them with formal certificates of service ; such documents are particularly useful in event of disputed pedigrees.

THE BROOD BITCH.

Young bitches often exhibit symptoms of an inclination to breed at the age of eight or nine months, but it is undesirable to place them at the stud until they have reached the age of at least eighteen months. The remarks we made above against the advisability of resorting to the services of too young a sire, apply with even greater force when a youthful bitch is under consideration. Stunted and puny puppies are almost sure to be produced from a young mother ; and the injury they are likely to do her constitution is incalculable. It must be borne in mind that for weeks before birth her system is sorely taxed to provide them with nourishment, and after the shock of labour is gone through there is a further strain upon her until they are weaned.

The first symptom afforded by a bitch that she is likely to be soon ready for breeding purposes, is a desire on her part to romp and play with any dog she meets. This may possibly arise from merely exuberance of spirits, but it is always well to keep a close eye upon her as soon as any undue levity is observed in her conduct. It is most desirable to use every endeavour to keep the animal away from all risk of being got at by strange dogs ; and when the matter is placed beyond doubt all former precautions should be doubled if possible. It must be remembered that there is not only a great risk of dogs getting into the place where the bitch is confined, but that she will probably be equally anxious to escape from her kennel, and some bitches have performed almost incredible feats in their endeavours to do so.

She should, if at a distance, be sent off to the kennels where the dog is standing a day or two after the earlier symptoms appear, so as to be in time. If despatched by public conveyance, it is imperative that she be securely confined in a box or basket from which escape is impossible. The transit of dogs has been more fully treated in the chapter on exhibiting, and need not be further alluded to here ; but all breeders should be impressed with the absolute necessity of exercising the greatest vigilance when they have bitches by them under such circumstances. For at least a week after the bitch has visited the dog, the precautions for isolating her must not be relaxed, or all her owner's hopes may be marred by her forming a connection with a stranger.

The influence of a previous sire on a subsequent litter of puppies is a subject of the keenest discussion and interest amongst breeders, and a most interesting correspondence has taken place in the columns of the *Live Stock Journal* relating thereto. Some of the statements which have appeared from time to time in that journal upon this subject, and which have been substantiated by the names of writers whose position as breeders of various varieties of live stock is assured, are invested with a peculiar importance. But having carefully read and considered the matter, we find ourselves driven back on the supposition that although such occurrences undoubtedly have arisen, they are not by any means the matter-of-course events some of the correspondents of the *Live Stock Journal* consider them, and in more than one instance we have failed to satisfy ourselves that the influences imputed have regulated the course of events. In making this statement we attribute to the writers no desire to impose on public credulity, but we think they have too often forgotten the influence which surrounding objects exercise over the mind of a pregnant female. This opinion is shared by many breeders of live stock, and it is notorious that a celebrated breeder of black polled cattle had his premises and fences tarred, with the express object of assisting Nature in keeping the colour of his stock as deep as possible. It is, however, quite impossible for us to go at length into the subject, and it must therefore be dismissed with the remark that as many breeders firmly believe, from personal experience, that such a thing as past influence is possible, especially in the case of maiden bitches, due vigilance should be exercised in the thorough isolation of bitches when in season, or more than a temporary evil and disappointment may occur

PUPPING.

Having selected a proper mate for his bitch, and sent her to him, all anxiety is removed from an owner's mind for some time at least ; for during the first period of going with young, the bitch will require no special diet or attention. It may be here stated, for the benefit of the uninitiated, that the period of gestation amongst dogs is sixty-three days, and that this time is rarely exceeded unless something is wrong, though it sometimes occurs that the whelps make their appearance some days before they are expected. During this period the bitch should be allowed plenty of exercise, but during the latter portion of her pregnancy she is peculiarly liable to chills ; every care should therefore be taken to avoid any risk of her taking cold, and all washing operations and *violent* exercise must then be suspended. Our own experience has taught us that in the majority of instances it is almost impossible to tell whether or no the bitch is in whelp until the third or fourth week, and on many occasions we have known breeders to be in doubt for a much longer period ; in fact, on discussing with a very well-known Pointer exhibitor the accouchement of one of his exhibits during a show, he assured us that when she left home she had shown no traces of being in whelp, and as a matter of fact her time was not up until the following week.

A week or so before the date on which it is expected that she will whelp, the bitch should be installed in the quarters in which it is arranged the interesting event is to take place. The reason for this is that dogs must get used to a kennel before they will make themselves at home in it, and this feeling is peculiarly perceptible in the case of a bitch who has recently whelped ; for in many cases she will try and carry her puppies (greatly to the damage of the latter) back to her old quarters rather than let them remain in a kennel to which she is unaccustomed. Having got her reconciled to her change of abode, the *locale* of which should, if possible, be away from the other dogs, so as to let her have more quiet (but *warmth* and *absence of draught* are even more essential than isolation in such cases), and supposing the time of her whelping to be near at hand, it is desirable that the bitch should be provided with a diet of a more strengthening character than that which she has been in the habit of receiving. This need not consist entirely of meat or other heating foods, which can only tend to increase her discomfort in parturition, but may be made of scraps well boiled or stewed, with the addition of bread, meal, or rice, which in their turn will absorb the gravy or soup, and form, in conjunction with the scraps, when the latter are chopped up, a meal which is both wholesome and nutritious. A few days before the puppies make their appearance a considerable change is usually perceptible in the bitch ; the presence of milk can be detected, and a considerable enlargement of the stomach takes place. Her behaviour too, clearly indicates that she is uneasy and in pain, and in many instances the appetite entirely fails, and the bowels become confined. In the latter case a mild purgative of either castor, linseed, or sweet oil must be given. The first-named remedy is sometimes too powerful an aperient for a bitch in such a condition, as, in the more delicate breeds especially, it is apt to cause severe straining, which would injure the puppies. Before resorting, therefore, to castor-oil, an experimental dose of either linseed or sweet oil might be administered, which, if it succeed in acting on the bowels, will have satisfactorily accomplished the owner's object; and as the lubricating power of all three oils is essentially the same, the internal organs will be equally benefited by either medicine.

Two or three days before the puppies are due a good bed of straw should be provided, and this should not be changed till the whelps are at least a week old ; for unnecessary attention will certainly worry the mother, and may cause her to destroy her offspring. The bed of straw should be placed on boards raised not higher than two or three inches from the ground ; in fact, the bitch during the last few weeks of going in whelp should not be allowed the opportunity of leaping up and down on and off a high bench. On no account should the bed be placed on a cold stone or brick flooring ; and even a carpet is objectionable, for the mother, in making her bed for the reception of her young, invariably removes all the bedding from underneath her, and piles it up at the sides in the shape of a nest. Her object in acting thus is to facilitate the operation of licking the puppies ; as she will within a few hours of parturition have all her whelps thoroughly cleansed and freed from any offensive adherent matter, being during their earlier puppyhood most attentive to the personal cleanliness of her offspring. This would be impossible if she allowed them to lie on the straw, as the wet would soak into it and cause the bed to become foul.

The different temperaments and dispositions of various bitches become specially apparent as parturition approaches. Some will be impatient at the slightest intrusion on the solitude they evidently prefer, whilst others eagerly welcome the familiar voice of master or attendant, and seem to beg him to remain beside them in the time of suffering. A great deal must therefore be left to the judgment of those in charge of the bitch ; but it should be borne in mind that, though an occasional visit is necessary even in the case of a most unsociably-disposed bitch, in order to see that nothing has gone wrong, still *too much* interference and fidgeting even with a quiet one is apt to render her feverish, and increase the difficulties of her situation. Under any circumstances a plentiful amount of cold water should always be placed near her, and beyond this she will, in the majority of instances, want nothing until the pups are born. Should she however become exhausted during labour, a little port wine may be given now and then. When safely delivered, some gruel should be given her, and she should be kept on this diet for the space of two or three days ; it is strengthening and soothing to the internal organs, and can be made either with milk or water; the addition of a little gravy or beef tea is an excellent practice after the first two or three basins of gruel. The quantity of gruel should be unlimited, and very often she will devour a basinful every two or three hours for the first day ; care, however, must be taken not to let it remain by her too long, so as to turn sour and disarrange the stomach, which it is very easy to do when a bitch has just whelped. It is always desirable to try and count the puppies when the mother is off the bed feeding, as it lets an owner know whether she eats her whelps or not ; and if he misses puppies he must try and devise some way to stop the proceeding.

In event of a puppy dying, it must of course be removed at the first opportunity offering itself, and if this can be managed without the knowledge of the mother, so much the better ; for we have known instances where a whole litter has been destroyed by a dam on the removal of one dead whelp from their midst ; and, besides this, there is the danger of a bite from a bad-tempered bitch if she sees her family carried off. Opinions vary much as regards whether dogs can count or not; but our own belief is decidedly in favour of their being able to do so up to a certain number. This is a matter of considerable importance where puppies are concerned, for it is often necessary to remove some from the mother. Some bitches seem to take no notice of the diminished number of their family, whilst others appear frenzied by their bereavement, and, acting on a first impulse, have destroyed the remaining whelps, unless restrained from doing so. It being therefore certain that mothers are capable of discovering, by counting or otherwise, when any of their puppies have been removed in their absence, it behoves the breeder to be careful how he acts when such a course has to be adopted. If he carefully watches the bitch for half an hour or so on her re-introduction to her family, and sees that all is well, he need have no further care on that score; but should she become restless, and show signs of an inclination to destroy the remaining whelps, she must be closely guarded in order to prevent mischief. Some bitches are notorious for the habit they have of killing their puppies, and in such cases the only means to adopt is, in the absence of a foster-mother, to take the puppies in-doors, and keep them warmly wrapped up in a basket lined with flannel before a fire, and let the mother come and suckle them every two hours. Whilst with them she should be laid on her side, and gently held down so as to prevent her injuring them in any way.

Having alluded above to the subject of foster-mothers, we may express the opinion that, in the event of valuable puppies being expected, the acquisition of such an animal is very desirable. A bitch in whelp can often be obtained from the Dogs' Home, Battersea, for a few shillings, and if one is not to be obtained there in a suitable condition of pregnancy, Mr. Scorborio, the courteous and energetic manager of that institution can often put owners in the way of obtaining one at a very reasonable figure. Foster-mothers can also frequently be hired for a few weeks, if advertised for in the papers; and as a matter of fact we once obtained the services of seven at £1 each from one advertisement in the *Live Stock Journal.* The greatest precaution must however be exercised by owners, in order that no diseased or unhealthy bitch be received in the responsible position of wet-nurse to their puppies, for the danger of such an introduction can hardly be exaggerated; and therefore many persons rather shrink from investing in bitches of whose antecedents they are ignorant.

Aid from inexperienced persons when administered to a bitch in labour is almost sure to be attended with most unsatisfactory results, and we are simply re-echoing the opinion of the vast majority of practical breeders when we express the conviction that many of the so-called veterinary surgeons practising in this country know next to nothing of canine pathology. A man who may or may not have passed his examination at the Veterinary College, and professes to be an adept at physicking horses or doctoring cows, invariably considers himself quite qualified to attend upon dogs, and possibly in a few cases he may be so; but in most instances he knows less than the kennel-man does, and increases the ailing dog's difficulties by his injudicious treatment. "There is a man down the street who knows all about dogs," is a common saying when the owner is in a difficulty, and the man is sent for, generally turning out to be absolutely incompetent and grossly ignorant of what he professes to understand. For our own part we believe that doctoring their own dogs is an easy task for tolerably intelligent and fairly attentive owners, and experience has taught us that the list of drugs and remedies which are applicable to canine diseases is a very limited one indeed, and that an elaborate doggy pharmacopœia is a wholly unnecessary institution, which can only tend to complicate the difficulties which lie in the way of a beginner when he attempts to arrive at a correct diagnosis and treatment of his animal's ailments. In cases of protracted labour, where there are indications of internal complications, surgical aid must of course be rendered the bitch, provided really competent professional assistance can be obtained. All other is useless in such cases, and we must once again impress upon our readers the terrible danger and torture to which they subject their dogs by calling in the assistance of incompetent advisers. *Be convinced that your surgeon knows more than you do yourself,* is a golden rule for breeders to lay heed to.

In the event of the bitch being unable to pass her puppies after being in labour for some time, the application of crushed ice to the abdomen is frequently the means of enabling her to do so, as it has the effect of contracting the muscles of the womb, and thus assists in the expulsion of the whelps. Ergot is sometimes used in complicated cases as a uterine excitant, but should be resorted to only as an extreme measure, being, in the hands of inexperienced persons, a very dangerous medicine. Oiling the vagina is also in many cases a relief to the bitch. In some books we have seen it strongly recommended as a means of assisting protracted labour that the bitch should be immersed in a warm bath for a few minutes; this in ninety-nine cases out of a hundred involves two certain results—(1) almost instant relief to the dog, (2) DEATH. According to the theory propounded by Mayhew in his work on canine diseases, the application of warm water causes a relaxation of the muscles of the womb, whereas an exactly opposite effect is needed; thus the temporary relief from her suffering costs the poor beast her life, and her owner the mortification of having killed her by improper treatment. We know not of one only, but of scores of such instances occurring; and no doubt all breeders of experience are well acquainted with the ill effects of an injudicious bath to a bitch in labour.

Some curiosity on the part of a youthful breeder is natural enough where the first puppies of his own breeding are concerned; but he will be acting very foolishly indeed if he gives way to it. It cannot be any advantage to him to discover the sexes of the different whelps on the day of their birth, and all handling should be avoided unless it is thought desirable to remove some from the mother on account of the number being considered too many for her to bring up. It should be borne in mind that four or five strong, vigorous, well-nourished puppies are far more likely to turn out satisfactorily for their owner than eight or ten scantily-nourished ones; and it must be left to the good sense of the breeder to decide, from the condition of the bitch and the amount of milk she has secreted, how many she can do justice to without injuring herself. Five or six are enough for a moderate-sized bitch, and eight or ten for a large one. The extra ones can be destroyed if sickly, or placed under a foster-mother, if one can be got. In some instances puppies have been very successfully brought up by hand, through the immediate agency of a baby's feeding bottle; but before any one enters upon such an undertaking due consideration should be devoted to the magnitude of the task before him. Constant feeding is necessary, and the whelps require a great deal of warmth, patience, and attention. In circumstances like this the most valuable ally of all is to be found in the cook; if her hearty co-operation is obtained the chances are that the whelps will go on and prosper, for a snug corner for the basket on the kitchen hearth, and the constant supervision she can give them, is sure to benefit them very considerably.

About the ninth day the puppies begin to open their eyes, and very soon they commence crawling out of their nest and about the floor of the kennel; after which it is wonderful how fast they seem to grow and the strength they display. At two weeks old they will commence to eat bread-and-gravy, or bread-and-milk, if it is provided for them, though the latter is, we think, an objectionable diet, as it is apt to turn sour, and also, if cow's milk, to breed worms, to which young puppies are peculiarly liable. Goat's milk, however, we consider good for puppies, as it, according to our experience, does not increase the risk of worms. During this time the food given to the mother should be of a strengthening nature, so as to enable her to stand the strain on her constitution which her maternal duties involve, but care should be taken to prevent her bringing bones into her bed, as many instances have occurred of mothers severely biting their puppies who have attempted to take the bones from her. One or two gentle runs a day are now very necessary for the bitch, as exercise not only freshens her considerably, but gives her a chance of getting away from the persistent persecution which the puppies inflict upon her. At five weeks old the whelps may usually begin to be removed from their mother, and it is well to do this gradually, as they suffer less from the separation if this course is pursued ; and by extending the intervals of the bitch's absence they can be almost entirely weaned without any ill effects to either themselves or their dam. The best method is to begin by removing the bitch for an hour or two in the warmest part of the day, so that the chance of the puppies catching cold is diminished. The periods of her absence can then be prolonged until she is only returned to them of a night, and finally ceases to visit them at all.

It frequently occurs that the teats of the bitch have been wounded by the teeth of the puppies when they suckle her ; and inflammation, from the influx of milk, often arises when they are removed. Considerable relief can be obtained by rubbing some camphorated oil well over her stomach, and this can be repeated night and morning for some days, a mild dose of physic being administered when the puppies are finally removed. In the event, however, of the milk that she has secreted still bothering her, and her teats being so tender that drawing some off by ordinary milking is impossible recourse may be had to an ordinary soda-water bottle, heated with hot water, the mouth of which can be pressed over the inflamed teat. This has the effect of drawing some of the milk out, and thereby relieving the bitch of a great deal of pain. Or an ordinary breast-pump may be employed.

Having now given a brief sketch of the general treatment of a bitch when pupping, we will pass on to the future management of the whelps themselves.

REARING.

On the removal of the whelps from their mother, a very considerable change for the worse immediately takes place in their appearance, which is due mainly to the alteration in their diet and general mode of life. Instead of drawing a certain amount of sustenance from their dam at the cost of no trouble, they are now cast upon their own resources for a means of subsistence. The necessity of having to get up and hunt about for the dish which contains its food is a fact which it takes a puppy's mind a long time to master. Consequently the entire litter often passes many hungry hours during the night, although their food is within a few inches of their bed ; and it is not until a happy thought strikes one of them that it might be a good plan if he got up and looked for something, that they all follow his example, and fall to as only hungry puppies can. Almost all puppies suffer greatly from worms, and immediately on their removal from their mother means should be taken to rid them of such torments. The presence of worms is certain when the stomachs of puppies swell and harden, but they frequently exist without developing such symptoms. It is therefore the safer plan to administer one or two doses of worm medicine all round, especial care being taken that their delicate mouths and throats are not injured in administering the remedy. The two best vermifuges are areca-nut and santonine. The latter, in its crystallised form, is an excellent remedy for worms in dogs, and about two grains in butter cannot be surpassed as a vermifuge for puppies of seven or eight weeks old, whose parents weigh from forty to sixty pounds weight. If too strong a dose is given, santonine has a tendency to affect the brain and cause fits, so precaution must be exercised in administering this medicine. The chief difficulty in the use of areca-nut lies in getting it freshly grated, as if allowed to become stale it loses its virtue as an anthelmintic. To avoid this the nut should be grated on an ordinary nutmeg-grater, and given immediately in butter or lard. The ordinary dose is two grains for every pound the dog weighs, but more than two drachms should never be given. Spratt's worm powders are also excellent remedies, if an owner has to clear his pets of these pests, and are easily procured of any chemist.

It is useless to resort to any remedy for worms in dogs unless the medicine is administered on an empty stomach. Small dogs should fast for at least twelve hours, and large powerful animals for twenty-four, before the medicine is administered. It is also desirable to prevent their drinking too much water during the period of their abstention, the object being to deprive the worms of all sorts of food, so that the anthelmintic may have a greater chance of success. Many persons give a dose of castor-oil the night before the vermifuge is given, and a second one two or three hours after if it has had no effect. As long as the purgative does not tax the dog's system too powerfully, these precautions materially assist the operation of the medicine; but judgment and caution must, of course, be exercised, and it would be foolish to adopt such vigorous treatment with a weakly puppy.

Crushed biscuits, oatmeal-porridge, and bread-and-gravy, with the addition of a little chopped meat and végetables, are the best diet for puppies when first away from their mother, and the amount they can get through in the course of twenty-four hours is considerable. The greatest care must be taken to guard against the puppies (this, in fact, applies to any dogs, but to puppies especially) being given food which is *sour or decomposed.'* A very fruitful and common cause of this has only lately come to our knowledge. We are indebted for the following information to Mr. F. Gresham, whose experience in feeding large dogs is very considerable. This gentleman has proved by experience that food cooked in a copper or other boiler is very apt to turn sour as soon as cooked, if allowed to stand and cool *in the vessel in which it has been prepared.* Care should therefore be taken to remove it, as soon as the culinary operations are completed, to a cool and clean receptacle, where it can remain until it is required for the dogs, or is returned to the boiler, to be added to other meals in course of preparation.

All draughts should be kept away from their kennel, which must be warm and dry, or the puppies will not spread and grow as they should do; and a run in a dry yard is imperative, if the weather is not too cold or damp. By keeping his puppies clean and dry, an owner considerably lessens the risk of distemper ravaging his kennels, for this fearful scourge is unquestionably amenable to sanitary arrangements, and except on very rare occasions, when its origin can usually be traced, is scarcely ever present in well-conducted establishments. In our own kennels we have never experienced a single case of distemper amongst puppies of our own breeding, and this has been under circumstances of great difficulty, where for over three years an average of nearly fifty dogs have been kept in confined spaces. A strict attention to cleanliness, fresh air, fresh water, sound food, combined with proper grooming and exercise, renders the presence of distemper well-nigh impossible, and if a breeder who attends to these matters has the misfortune to have it communicated to his stock (for distemper *is* contagious), he will find them the better able to resist its attacks if they have been previously well looked after.

Our own treatment in the few cases we had in cases of puppies we had bought (one or two of which sickened within the week) were thorough and absolute isolation in the first place, so as to preclude all possibility of contagion or infection in case of other diseases. We had a lumber-room attached to the house cleared for a hospital, and fitted with a gas stove; by this means a steady even temperature can be maintained night and day, and this is a most important feature in the treatment of distemper. All stuffiness in the air should be avoided, for it must be remembered that in this disease the nostrils become charged with a thick fluid which renders breathing very difficult. We invariably had the window open at the top, and with the gas stove aided by a thermometer kept the room at a steady temperature of 60 degrees. The only food given was beef-tea with some bread soaked in it, and the only medicine Rackham's distemper pills. Seeing is believing, and we believe these pills to be almost infallible in the treatment of distemper, never having lost a dog when using them, and knowing many breeders who share our opinion, we cannot resist alluding to them. When the graver symptoms begin to subside solid food can be administered, and the dog picks up wonderfully soon, though too premature an introduction to the cold outside is to be deprecated after his confinement so long in a warm temperature. A friend—we rather think it was Mr. R. Fulton, of Brockley—once told us of a food which he considered a capital change for dogs suffering from distemper, and this was a number of fresh haddocks' heads put into a pot and covered with water, to be boiled until the bones of the fish get soft and the water is almost entirely absorbed; this, when cold, forms a jelly, which is keenly appreciated by the invalids, and seems to do them good. Our friend's theory was that the phosphorus contained in the fish-bones assisted the medicine in curing the dog; but be this as it may, it is certain that no ill effects, but rather the contrary, resulted from giving it them.

Allusion having thus been made to the two greatest plagues of puppyhood—worms and distemper—there hardly remain more diseases to which they are peculiarly liable. Fits they certainly often suffer from, but these almost invariably are the result of worms, and will subside and disappear when the irritating cause of their presence is removed. Teething occasionally troubles them, but seldom to any great extent, for puppies do not usually shed their first teeth until nine months old, and then they are strong enough to bear the pain and annoyance the cutting of their new ones inflicts upon them. Should the puppies, however, appear to suffer from the swelling of their gums previous to the appearance of a tooth, it is well to lance the inflamed part, especially if the gum appears abnormally hard. Not only does this give immediate relief, but it helps the teeth to come up in a regular line, which in most varieties is most desirable.

The exercise and subsequent treatment of the whelps have been so thoroughly gone into in the chapters on general management and exercise, that no further allusion to them is requisite here.

LACTOL

— FOR —

Weaning and Rearing
Puppies and Kittens.

NO COOKING REQUIRED—JUST ADD HOT WATER.
HUNDREDS OF UNSOLICITED TESTIMONIALS RECEIVED.
USED IN ALL THE LEADING KENNELS.

THE most critical stage of a puppy's existence is the weaning period—from five to eight weeks old—when he is taken from the dam. Until the introduction of Lactol, puppies, as a general rule, were weaned on unsuitable foods, most unlike the mother's milk that they have but shortly left, with the result that they invariably suffered from indigestion, diarrhœa, vomiting, distended stomach, &c., and in many cases died.

An analysis of the milk of a bitch shows immediately why this should be the case, as it is seen to be three times as strong as cow's or goat's milk. The only food on which puppies can be safely weaned and reared is Lactol, which, when mixed with hot water as directed, forms a food three times as strong as cow's milk, and identical in taste, analysis, and appearance with the puppy's natural food.

It is regularly used and recommended by all the leading dog fanciers and canine specialists, and is most highly spoken of by the veterinary and kennel press.

In Tins, 1/-, 2/6, 5/- and 20/-.

Of BOOTS', TAYLOR'S DRUG CO., WHITELEY'S, HARRODS, ARMY & NAVY STORES, and other leading Stores and Chemists, or from the Manufacturers :—

A. F. SHERLEY & CO., 46 & 48, BOROUGH HIGH ST., S.E.

The Kennel Library.

BRITISH DOGS.

Their Points, Selection, and Show Preparation. Third Edition. By eminent specialists. Beautifully Illustrated. This is the fullest work on the various breeds of dogs kept in England. In one volume, *demy 8vo, cloth, price 12/6 nett, by post 13/-.*

PRACTICAL KENNEL MANAGEMENT.

A Complete Treatise on the Proper Management of Dogs, for the Show Bench, the Field, or as Companions, with a chapter on Diseases—their Causes and Treatment. By well-known Specialists. Illustrated. *In cloth, price 10/6 nett, by post 11/-.*

DISEASES OF DOGS.

Their Causes, Symptoms, and Treatment; Modes of Administering Medicines; Treatment in cases of Poisoning, &c. For the use of Amateurs. By HUGH DALZIEL. Fourth Edition. Entirely Re-written and brought up to date. By ALEX. C. PIESSE, M.R.C.V.S. *Price 1/- nett, by post 1/2; in cloth, price 2/- nett, by post 2/3.*

BREAKING AND TRAINING DOGS.

Being Concise Directions for the proper education of Dogs, both for the Field and for Companions. Second Edition. By "PATHFINDER." Many new Illustrations. *In cloth, price 6/6 nett, by post 6/10.*

POPULAR DOG KEEPING:

Being a Handy Guide to the General Management and Training of all Kinds of Dogs for Companions and Pets. Third Edition. By J. MAXTEE. Illustrated. *Price 1/- nett, by post 1/2.*

THE FOX TERRIER.

Its Points, Breeding, Rearing, Preparing for Exhibition. Second Edition, Revised and brought up to date. Fully Illustrated. *Price 1/- nett, by post 1/2.*

THE COLLIE,

As a Show Dog, Companion, and Worker. Revised by J. MAXTEE. Third Edition. Illustrated. *Price 1/- nett, by post 1/2.*

THE GREYHOUND:

Its Points, Breeding, Rearing, Training, and Running. Second Edition, Revised and brought up to date by J. MAXTEE, assisted by T. B. RIXON. Illustrated. *Price 1/- nett, by post 1/2.*

THE WHIPPET OR RACE-DOG.

How to Breed, Rear, Train, Race, and Exhibit the Whippet, the Management of Race Meetings, and Original Plans of Courses. By FREEMAN LLOYD. Illustrated. *Price 1/- nett, by post 1/2.*

BREEDERS' AND EXHIBITORS' RECORD,

For the Registration of Particulars concerning Pedigree Stock of every Description. By W. K. TAUNTON. In three parts. *In cloth, price each 2/6 nett, or the set 6/- nett, by post 6/6.*

Part I., The Pedigree Record.   Part II., The Stud Record.

Part III., The Show Record.

London : L. UPCOTT GILL, Bazaar Buildings, Drury Lane, W.C.

Kennel Indispensables.

The Ideal Disinfectant

Famous as a cure for Mange, Eczema, Ringworm, and all other parasitic skin diseases.

A GRAND HAIR PRODUCER.

Destroys all insects such as fleas, lice, ticks, etc.

Sold in tins at 9d., 1/3, 2/- each; 6/- per gallon.
Free for P.O.

The Kennel, the Stable, the Poultry Yard kept sweet and healthy.
Ask for IZAL Veterinary Pamphlet.

IZAL Disinfectant Powder.

THE STRONGEST POWDER KNOWN.

In tins, 6d. and 1/- each; 50 lb. casks, 5/-. Free for P.O.

IZAL Soft Soap, *8d. per lb. Post free.*
IZAL Bar Soap. *8d. per lb. Post free.*

Special quotations for large lots.

NEWTON, CHAMBERS & Co., Ltd.,
THORNCLIFFE, NEAR SHEFFIELD.

BARNARDS LIMITED, NORWICH

IMPROVED RANGE OF KENNELS AND RUNS.
No. 347.

Each kennel, 6ft. wide, 5ft. deep. Runs, each 6ft. long, 6ft. wide, finished in the very best style.

One House and Run	**£7 10 0**
Two Houses and Runs	**12 15 0**
Three ditto	**18 18 0**
Six ditto	**35 0 0**
Carriage Paid.	

NEW PORTABLE KENNEL AND RUN.
Registered Design.
No. 345.

3ft. 6in. wide, 8ft. long, 4ft. high	**£4 5 0**
4ft. wide, 9ft. 6in. long, 5ft. high	**5 10 0**
5ft. wide, 12ft. long, 5ft. high	**7 10 0**
Carriage Paid.	

IMPROVED KENNEL.
No. 348.

AWARDED GOLD MEDAL SCHEVENINGEN, 1901 and 1906.

For Terriers ...	**£1 7 6**
For Collies, &c.	**2 5 6**
For Mastiffs ...	**3 9 6**
Carriage Paid.	

LEAN-TO PORTABLE KENNEL AND RUN.
No. 346

House, 4ft. by 3ft. 6in. Run, 4ft. by 6ft.

Cash Price	**£5 0 0**
Wood Back for Run,	**22/6** extra.
Corrugated Iron round Run	**5/-** extra.
Reversible Trough	**5/-**
Carriage Paid.	

CATALOGUE FREE:
Norfolk Iron Works, Norwich.

CPSIA information can be obtained at www.ICGtesting.com
Printed in the USA
LVOW041801261111

256568LV00001B/213/A